A TIFFANY CHRISTMAS

A Tiffany Christmas

JOHN LORING

DOUBLEDAY

New York   London   Toronto

Sydney   Auckland

ALSO BY *John Loring*

The Tiffany Wedding

Tiffany's 150 Years

Tiffany Taste

The New Tiffany Table Settings
   (with Henry B. Platt)

Tiffany Parties

The Tiffany Gourmet Cookbook

PUBLISHED BY DOUBLEDAY
a division of Bantam Doubleday Dell Publishing Group, Inc.
1540 Broadway, New York, New York 10036

DOUBLEDAY and the portrayal of an anchor
with a dolphin are trademarks of Doubleday,
a division of Bantam Doubleday Dell
Publishing Group, Inc.

Book design by Marysarah Quinn

Excerpts from *A Child's Christmas in Wales* by Dylan Thomas
reprinted by permission of Harold Ober Associates and New
Directions Publishing Corp. Copyright © 1954.
Excerpt from "Christmas Card to Grace Hartigan" from *Collected
Poems* by Frank O'Hara © 1971 by Maureen Grainville-Smith,
Administratrix of the Estate of Frank O'Hara. Reprinted by
permission of Alfred A. Knopf Inc.
Excerpts from *A Carol for Children* from *Verses from 1929* by Ogden
Nash. Copyright © 1934 Ogden Nash, renewed; first appeared in *The
New Yorker.* Reprinted by permission of Curtis Brown, Ltd., and
Little, Brown and Company.
Excerpts from *The Snow Queen, The Little Match Girl, The Fir Tree,*
and *The Loveliest Rose in the World* by Hans Christian Andersen
reprinted by permission of Reed Consumer Books.

Library of Congress Cataloging-in-Publication Data
Loring, John.
   A Tiffany Christmas / John Loring. — 1st ed.
     p.   cm.
   1. Table setting and decoration. 2. Tableware. 3. Christmas
decorations. 4. Tiffany and Company. I. Title.
TX879.L67   1996
642′.6—dc20
                                  96-13534
                                      CIP

ISBN 0-385-48585-9

10   9   8   7   6   5   4   3   2   1

FIRST EDITION

ACKNOWLEDGMENTS

Tiffany & Co. would like to thank William R. Chaney, who as Chairman of the Board has presided over fourteen years of Christmases at Tiffany's; Nelsea Duncan, Director of Tiffany's table display department, for her incomparable expertise in the creation of Tiffany table settings over more than a quarter of a century; Billy Cunningham for his magnificent photography; Bruce Newman of Newel Antiques, who has kept the doors of his Aladdin's cave of so stylish treasures of the decorative arts open at all times to Tiffany's to furnish Tiffany's table setting shows for the past eighteen years; John Funt, who contributed so many festive ideas on party décor; Sir Humphrey Wakefield for orchestrating the participation of the many great Stately Homes of England and Scotland and for enlisting the support of Baker Furniture and their Stately Homes Collection, which Sir Humphrey created; Rollins Maxwell, Kay Freeman, Nicholas Arjona and Eric Armstrong for their insightful research on the evolution of Christmas as it is known today; Eric Erickson, who served as traffic warden and gave invaluable aesthetic counsel; and MaryAnn Aurora, who kept order throughout this project; and, of course, our editor Bruce Tracy for his enthusiasm and understanding.

Special thanks go to the late Jacqueline Kennedy Onassis, who edited the first six Doubleday-Tiffany books and without whose past guidance neither John Loring nor Bruce Tracy could have produced *A Tiffany Christmas.*

Contents

Tiffany & Co. "Holly and Mistletoe" Christmas silver, 1890s.

INTRODUCTION

As celebrated as Tiffany's Christmas windows, displays and table settings are today, when the original Tiffany store at 259 Broadway first opened its doors for business on September 21, 1837, it was not with the twentieth-century merchant's vision of a busy Christmas season on the way. In 1837, it would still be a few years before New Yorkers would observe Christmas as a time for celebration and as a time for the exchange of gifts. New York's merchants did not lay in stocks of presents for the "holiday season," and Charles Lewis Tiffany was at work on December 25, 1837, a business-as-usual day on lower Broadway. The next year, 1838, Christmas Day business at Tiffany's netted only $236.90 in sales.

The United States was more than slow in departing from its puritanical origins. And in the 1830s Americans generally felt that the Cromwellian Act of Parliament of August 26, 1645, which made it a punishable crime in England or its colonies to celebrate Christmas with feasting and revelry, was still in effect. Whatever public enthusiasm there was in New York for what has now become the holiday season went no further than the exchange of rather modest New Year's Day gifts.

Of course, Christmas celebrations are not in any way a modern invention. They have eminently respectable and ancient origins, even if the majority of those origins have nothing to do with Christmas and have everything to do with age-old pagan observances of the winter solstice and the beginning of the new year.

By tradition, Christmas celebrations first came to England as an idea of the fourth-century Pope Julius I, who instructed his lieutenants to convert pagan Britain's traditional winter solstice festival to a Christian celebration. On coming to the papacy in 337, Julius I had settled on December 25 as an expedient date to celebrate Christ's birthday. The integration of this official, if historically undocumented date—conveniently tucked between the winter solstice and New Year's—was intended by the Pope to do little to disturb the Britons' or the Romans' customary celebrations.

Pagan Britain's Norse/Viking Juul, honoring the resurrecting solar god, Woden, began on December 21, the shortest day of the year, the winter solstice, and lasted until January 1. This coincided nicely with the Romans' traditional Saturnalia festival of rejuvenation, where the god of agriculture was encouraged to chase winter away as quickly as possible so that the world might be reborn in the spring. The Saturnalia ended with the Kalendea, the Romans' gift-giving occasion at the outset of the new "calendar" year.

The garlands, wreaths and red-berried greenery brought into homes for the winter solstice festivities, it is reasonable to assume, changed little in their conversion to Christian usage in either Rome or Britain, and holly with its red berries played its symbolic role in both cultures. The public, in any case, seemed to care little whether they were celebrating Saturn, Woden or Christ as long as they were celebrating.

From the fourth century on, the Yule or Christmas/New Year's revelry continued uninterrupted in England until the reformer Oliver Cromwell and his fun-hating Puritan associates outlawed Christmas celebrations as pagan and "popish," and therefore "Roman," which, of course, they were.

If this was not dampening enough to the Christmas/New Year's spirit, three and one half years later Cromwell sent a grisly warning to those still given to fun and revelry by having England's notoriously festivity-loving Catholic King Charles I summarily beheaded in front of the newly built banqueting hall of his Whitehall Palace on the chilly morning of January 30, 1649.

This very unmerry Christmas situation lingered on for eleven not-at-all-festive years until 1660 and the restoration of Charles I's son, Charles II, to the English throne, with the ensuing repeal of Puritan laws. A popular almanac of the time proclaimed, "Now thanks to God for Charles' return whose absence made old Christmas mourn."

Notwithstanding, old Christmas remained a "mourn" affair after Cromwell and the Puritans, and it was only during the reign of Queen Victoria nearly two hundred years later that a wholesale revival of the old, traditional celebration came to England via Victoria's German consort, Prince Albert of Saxe-Coburg-Gotha. From there, the new, germanized Christmas came in turn to America, where Puritanism had curiously thrived far better than in its own native England.

Naturally, differences of opinion abound as to the clearly inexact origins of the Christmas traditions and images we know today.

The popularity of Christmas carols and caroling evolved from Britain's wassailing time at the outset

Tiffany pattern for a silver Christmas cup, 1875.

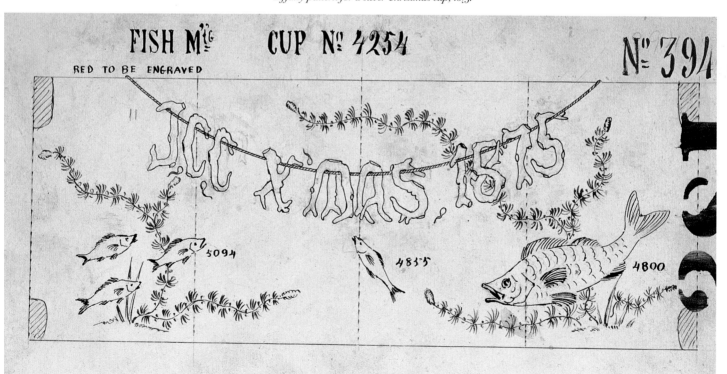

Tiffany Christmas card designs by Andy Warhol, late 1950s.

of January, when bands of revelers would go about the town and countryside singing and making as much noise as humanly possible on drums and pipes and anything they could crash together to chase off the evil spirits of the long winter nights. This jolly activity was inevitably assured of success. The nights had already begun to get shorter since the winter solstice on December 21, and for this the wassailers would take total credit.

To encourage prolonging the revels, the merry-makers would drink hot mixtures of sherry or sweet wine, ale, apples and lemons, all spiced with cloves, cinnamon and nutmeg—not unlike today's hot wine punches—while cheering each other with the more Saxon than Angle greeting of "Waes haeil," which roughly means "Good health."

The Christmas tree, with its supporting cast of holly, ivy and mistletoe, has many possible origins, as decorated and illuminated trees of one form or another appear throughout recorded history.

All variations on the theme of greenery, ornamented naturally or otherwise, were symbols of fertility and the happily anticipated renewal of life after the winter. The hedonistic ancient Romans preferred simple holly with its red berries. The Anglo-Saxons used holly too; however, they preferred mistletoe, with its white berries symbolizing a purer

form of love and regeneration at Yule time than the Romans had in mind during the Saturnalia and Kalendea, when visions of regeneration could get rowdily out of hand.

The tree itself was first, like the holly berries, another symbol of fire or knowledge having been stolen from the gods and given to man. Whether it derived from Loki, the reptilian god of lightning of primitive man, striking a tree and introducing us to fire; or from Prometheus the Titan, stealing the gods' flames so that we might feast like them; or from the shiny zigzag garland of the Devil disguised as a snake on Eden's apple-laden Tree of Knowledge; or from the ubiquitous Tree of Life, we will never know for sure; but then, it is of little importance. As a festive symbol of regeneration, the decorated and illuminated tree has endured for thousands of years.

The menorah itself, of the Jewish Hanukkah festival, is, of course, a nine-branched illuminated tree-inspired candleholder; and Hanukkah, although a movable feast, frequently falls very near the winter solstice.

The all-Amerian Christmas tree as such, however, is well documented as a direct descendant of the first "modern" Christmas tree, set up by Queen Victoria and Prince Albert at Windsor Castle in 1848 and pic-

tured in the *Illustrated London News*, a magazine then popular in the United States as well as in England. Our American Christmas has, in fact, kept quite close to its Victorian English origins.

Santa Claus, or Father Christmas, was not part of Victoria and Albert's Christmas, and did not appear either at Windsor Castle or in New York in 1848. His quite shady early lineage has led historians to propose, probably rightly, an evolution from ancient fur-clothed shaman or medicine man/magician/ keeper-of-the-flame figures, or even from the Germanic god Wöden's handyman/helper Eckhard.

In any case, a shaman ("dressed all in fur from his head to his foot") or merely a "jolly old elf" among Wöden's helpers who emerged from the legends of the Northern forests, Santa remains a joyously pagan reveler at Christmas festivities, one who children still believe flies through the air in a sleigh rather than on the less festive, if freedom-symbolizing, broom of lesser good- or ill-natured goblins. And his shaman's horns or antlers, of course, are now transferred to the reindeer who pull his sleigh.

Of these deer, there was usually only one until the American poet Clement Clarke Moore came to Santa's rescue in 1823 with the "eight tiny reindeer" of *A Visit from St. Nicholas*. Moore, however, still

left St. Nick "all tarnished with ashes and soot" like the old pagan apprentice of the sun god; and it was to be almost a century before he got his bright red, fur-trimmed costume.

Moore's mixed pagan and Christian references in his famous poem are all quite intentional. Moore was a noted scholar, the son of the second Episcopal bishop of New York and a professor of Hebrew at New York's General Theological Seminary. His universally popular poem takes ample account of the traditional Dutch Sinterklaas, who was part Lord of Misrule and part mythical St. Nicholas, the patron saint of the Dutch sailors who founded New York as New Amsterdam in 1625. It also takes account of more English pagan traditions.

As first illustrated, Moore's St. Nick was a funny little Dutchman dancing a jig and smoking a pipe, with toys spilling from his backpack. Then some forty years later, the German-born illustrator Thomas Nast redrew him as a slightly friendlier fur-clad German gnome, but it wasn't until 1931 that the Coca-Cola Company commissioned Haddon Sundblom to revise Santa, and so was born the jolly old fat Santa with his red suit and its white fur trim we know and love today.

If there was still any possibility of Santa's being

an authentic Christian personality, thirty-nine years after the new and improved, user-friendly Coca-Cola Santa came into being, Vatican II removed St. Nicholas from the roster of Catholic saints, confirming that his origins were purely mythic and founded in pagan tradition—something no one any longer doubted.

And here we are today with the Christmas holiday season restored to most of the mixed pagan and other religious and barbaric splendors of its decorated, illuminated trees, its wreaths and garlands, its hanging mistletoe, its blazing Yule logs and their pastry counterparts, its carols, its special foods for its feasts, its exchanges of gifts and greeting cards, its stockings hung by chimneys, its poems and stories, its shaped cookies and snowmen, its reindeer and Santas, its ribbons and colorful wrappings on gift boxes, and most of all its goodwill to absolutely everyone.

What role did Tiffany & Co. play in all this? We like to think a big one.

Probably our best chronicle of the arrival of Christmas decorations and celebrations in America comes from George Templeton Strong, a prominent Wall Street lawyer in the 1840s and '50s.

His diary entry for December 25, 1840, complains about "dissenters" (meaning puritanical Victorian Americans) who still opposed the celebration of Christmas, as though Cromwell's law of 1645 were still in effect:

Alas for schismatic city [New York], but few among its churches were open today. One would think that even if the matter of fact dissenters did consider it not quite demonstrably certain that this is the anniversary it professes to be, and if papaphobic dissenters did esteem its celebration a relic of popery, they wouldn't

be quite blind to all its glorious associations, quite oblivious that from all corners of Christendom the anthem of Thanksgiving rises this day unanimously.

A change in New York seems to have occurred the next year, for on December 25, 1841, Strong wrote that Christmas was "verily well observed— that's encouraging." Further encouragement came with the appearance of the penny post in 1840 and the first Christmas cards a few years later; not to mention the appearance in 1843 of Charles Dickens's *A Christmas Carol*, which can legitimately be credited with restoring the celebration of Christmas to the entire English-speaking world, as well as with proposing a new image of Father Christmas with the description of the Ghost of Christmas Present, even if Dickens's Spirit was dressed not in red but in "deep green":

"I am the Ghost of Christmas Present," said the Spirit. "Look upon me!" . . .

It was clothed in one simple deep green robe or mantle, bordered with white fur. This garment hung so loosely on the figure, that its capacious breast was bare, as if disdaining to be warded or concealed by any artifice. Its feet, observable beneath the ample folds of the garment, were also bare; and on its head it wore no other covering than a holly wreath, set here and there with shining icicles. Its dark brown curls were long and free: free as its genial face, its sparkling eye, its open hand, its cheery voice, its unconstrained demeanour, and its joyful air. Girded round its middle was an antique scabbard; but no sword was in it, and the ancient sheath was eaten up with rust.

"You have never seen the like of me before!" exclaimed the Spirit.

No one, indeed, prior to 1843 had seen the likes of him.

Strong did not write again about Christmas until 1853, when he was married, had two young children and lived on Gramercy Park. The Strongs gave and received presents on that Christmas Eve, when Strong's wife, Ellie, set up a table with presents and Christmas greens in the nursery. In 1854, she set up the table in the middle parlor downstairs.

In 1857, the Strongs' six-year-old son gave Ellie "a little silver brooch I got at Tiffany's on my way uptown and laboriously printed the inscription on its case—'Mama from Johnnie'—his first communication of a fact by written language . . ."

The Strongs were staunch Republicans, and on Christmas Eve in 1859, Ellie put up a large Christmas tree decorated with a flag bearing the inscription THE UNION FOREVER.

Starting in 1863, the Strongs exchanged presents on Christmas mornings after breakfast and before going to church.

In 1869, Strong's children had grown up and his thoughts turned to Ellie:

December 23   Walked uptown this afternoon Christmassing. Broadway flocked with folk on the same errand. Was weak enough to stop at Tiffany's, resolving to be parsimonious this year and spend not more than $20 on a pre-

sent for Ellie. But I was inflamed by a pretty cameo brooch, and involved myself to the extent of $200, which was sensible of me, especially so as had been obliged to subtract a little more capital from Trust Co. this morning to pay current bills. Never mind, I won't do it again, and I think Ellie will be much pleased by this bit of wampum . . .

Since George Templeton Strong chronicled the first American celebrations of Christmas and his purchases of gifts from Tiffany's in the 1850s and '60s, so many generations of Americans have delighted in finding a robin's-egg-blue box tied with a red satin ribbon among their own gifts, and to find Tiffany greeting cards in the mail.

Exactly two days after the twentieth anniversary of Strong's Christmas purchase from Tiffany's of the cameo for his wife, the *New York Times* chronicled a more lavish Christmas observance in its issue of December 25, 1889:

A UNIQUE
SURPRISE PARTY
A CHRISTMAS EVE
ENTERTAINMENT AT
MRS. ASTOR'S HOUSE

A surprise party was given Mrs. William Astor last night by about a hundred of her friends. Under the leadership of Mrs. Bradley Martin they drove from the latter's house, 22 West Twentieth Street, to the Astors' residence, 350 Fifth Avenue. They were fantastically arrayed. The ladies wore white satin dominos trimmed with holly, and the gentlemen each made a Santa Claus of himself, all being cloaked in long brown mantles and wearing caps trimmed with white fur. [Here was still the old, rather colorless Santa of the nineteenth century.]

By a piece of strategy the ballroom had

been elaborately decorated without Mrs. Astor's knowledge. There were masses of holly everywhere, and snowballs of white carnations and white violets almost completely covered the candelabra. In the alcove between the ballroom and the dining room was suspended a big snow-capped and fur-mantled Santa Claus with a remarkably jovial face.

Two rows of thirty-six small silk and satin stockings of varied colors were stretched across the ebony fireplace, and the representatives of Santa Claus filled them with bonbons and toys of all descriptions. A large bough of mistletoe hung from the balcony.

Immediately after their arrival the thirty-six couples began a cotillion, which was led by Henry Le Grand Cannon and Mrs. Martin. The first part was danced in costume. One of the unique figures was the distributing of favors by Mr. Cannon. He pushed about the ballroom a floral sleigh of smilax and holly, bound with broad ribbons of red, green and yellow. In it were the favors, consisting of miniature Santa Clauses, harlequins, and all sorts of dainty toys. Supper was served at 12:30, and after it the cotillion resumed . . .

The guest list of the Astor Christmas surprise party reads like Tiffany's client list of the period: Mr. and Mrs. William Waldorf Astor, Mr. and Mrs. John Jacob Astor, Jr., Mr. and Mrs. Cornelius Vanderbilt, Mr. and Mrs. F. W. Vanderbilt, Mr. and Mrs. Ogden Goelet, Mr. and Mrs. Seward Webb, Miss Winthrop, Miss Post, and so on.

Tiffany's had made the Astors' and the Vanderbilts' private flat-silver patterns for the table furnishings at their dinners and balls; had made trophies like the Goelet Cup for their schooner races; and had ornamented the ladies with the ex–Empress Eugénie of France's diamonds bought by Charles Lewis Tiffany the year before, in 1888, from republican France's Ministry of Finance. Did their Christmas gifts come from Tiffany's—undoubtedly they did.

A Tiffany Christmas has taken so many forms over Tiffany's now almost 160 years. There have been gifts ranging from sterling silver bicycles to diamonds from the crown jewels of France, to solid-gold tea and coffee services, to lifelike enameled and jeweled orchids, to Tiffany Favrile glass vases, to clocks with diamond hands, to the first kunzite, tanzanite and tsavorite jewels sold in America, to Elsa Peretti hearts, to Jean Schlumberger's gem-encrusted sea creatures, to Paloma Picasso's jeweled X's, and on to boxes of Tiffany Christmas cards designed by Andy Warhol.

Every holiday season, Tiffany's devotes its finest efforts to offering the tens of thousands of visitors to its famous New York store, at Fifth Avenue and Fifty-seventh Street, Christmas and holiday settings resplendent with Tiffany's legendary table furnishings and all the rich-textured trappings of the season's celebratory mood.

A Tiffany Christmas is our treasury of these settings, collected over many years, filled with our visions of celebrations both traditional and not so traditional, and it is our way of saying,

"Happy Holidays to all, and a very MERRY CHRISTMAS!"

John Loring
February 9, 1996

A Tiffany Christmas

BAKING CHRISTMAS CAKES

Christmas is a bright and splendid apparatus built of cookies and cakes and candies, mirrored glass balls, ribbons and garlands and anything red and green or reflective that can be pressed into service.

Great portions of joy are served up by the preparation of its edible decorations. Christmas gingerbread houses must be built by cooks, not by contractors, and the Christmas populace of cookies shaped like reindeer, Santas and snowmen all issue from the kitchen, where baking is the order of the day. Here young imaginations run wild putting frosting scribbles on every comestible surface; and each must discover whether almonds or candied cherries make better noses than buttons and whether raisins or jelly beans are most appropriate for eyes.

In the days before Christmas, "nonpareils," cinnamon hearts, foil-wrapped candies and stripy peppermints rain down on frosted gingerbread roofs, and everything has a delicious smell of candied fruits and spices.

Here a toy dog investigates the qualities of the Tiffany faience checkerboard tray of gingerbread men with a dog's usual attitude of temporarily baffled but hopeful curiosity, which is entirely shared by the white porcelain stag tureen overseeing the day's activities.

A diverse collection of Tiffany ceramics have been called into service; and to further animate the scene, two little angels dance around the kitchen's ceramic stovepipe.

> *"Tomorrow the kind of work I like best begins: buying. Cherries and citron, ginger and vanilla and canned Hawaiian pineapple, rinds and raisins and walnuts and whiskey and oh, so much flour, butter, so many eggs, spices, flavorings: why, we'll need a pony to pull the buggy home."*
>
> —TRUMAN CAPOTE,
> *A Christmas Memory*, 1956

DECO THE HALLS

At precisely the stroke of midnight, when December 31 of the old year unquietly becomes January 1 of the new, there is an outburst of extroversion quite unlike anything else in the whole festive procession of the holiday celebrations. Everyone embraces everyone else, and spiraling streamers of bright-colored paper fly through the air. As much noise is made as is humanly, mechanically and electronically possible; and enough champagne is consumed to keep France in luxuries for the next six months.

Precisely seven days before, on Christmas Eve, church bells chime out the arrival of Christmas as the twenty-fourth becomes the twenty-fifth of December, and a similarly animated celebration begins. A happy coincidence of tradition makes the exchange of gifts appropriate on both midnight occasions.

Here in a contemporarily urban and urbanely Deco setting, a totally "now" city dweller's ritual Christmas offerings of snow-white orchids and passionately red amaryllises arrive fresh for the celebrations.

There is hardly need for ornament beyond the colorfully celebratory company of Tiffany's "Cabaret" china, originally designed by Frank Lloyd Wright for Tokyo's Imperial Hotel in 1922. However, the sleek and debonair surfaces of the apartment's patterned tropical wood and sycamore American Deco furnishings are enlivened by Elsa Peretti–designed "Padova" sterling flat silver, Tiffany clocks to announce midnight, and a dapper "Metropolis" crystal decanter for Christmas spirits.

> " 'Keep Christmas in your own way, and let me keep it in mine.' "
> —CHARLES DICKENS, *A Christmas Carol*, 1843

PLANNING THE BALL

Since being introduced to Europe from Mexico in the late sixteenth century, the turkey triumphantly holds its own on Christmas dinner tables—Tiny Tim's matchless goose notwithstanding.

Curiously, however, of all the fowls displaced by King Turkey who once so generously offered themselves up stuffed and roasted at Christmastime, such as the humble goose, the regal swan and even the glorious peacock, the chicken and the rooster were never among them. It was not that their simple barnyard origins lacked adequate cachet for so noble a role, but folkloric tradition has it that the rooster crows all night from midnight to dawn on Christmas to welcome in the festive day; and for that these lucky fowl, were spared roasting.

The presence here of "great white fowls" from Tiffany's Italian ceramic collections comes then as no surprise on this buffet table set by Palm Beach and New York hostess Mrs. Michael ("Betsy") Kaiser for a planning committee luncheon preparatory to a December charity ball.

The discussions will be as lively as the lunch will be light. There will be cold curried pumpkin soup, a mixed salad topped with tomatoes and fresh mozzarella, homemade whole-grain bread, breadsticks and two sorbets, black chocolate and mandarin orange. A light red-wine punch will be served from a Tiffany "Cane Cut" crystal bowl.

A single oversized Tiffany "Baluster" Venetian crystal candlestick, wreathed with juniper, holly and bittersweet, ornaments the table; and to carry out the bird motifs, little scarlet-feathered cardinal ornaments flutter about in the traditionally decorated Christmas tree. Lunch will be eaten with Tiffany's bird-motif "Audubon" flat silver, a favorite since 1871.

> *"The snow-flakes became larger and larger; at last they looked*
> *like great white fowls."*
>
> —HANS CHRISTIAN ANDERSEN, *The Snow Queen*, 1846

CONNECTICUT YANKEE HOLIDAY

Christmas feasts, as known today, are recent inventions. Throughout much of early nineteenth-century New England, feasting on Christmas was considered nothing short of a criminal, pagan self-indulgence; the law sternly forbade it. Such Puritanism quickly changed in the last and more celebratory half of the nineteenth century; but a typical Yankee Christmas repast of the 1850s would have been marked by propriety bordering on pinched restraint rather than by exuberance bordering on debauch.

Here a classic mid-nineteenth-century New England table is laid with a certain hospitable air of ordered confusion, demonstrating the period's penchant for letting the picturesque take over from a colonial mix of Georgian and Regency neoclassicism and chinoiserie.

A gilt-and-black-lacquer neoclassic Regency chair teams up with an eighteenth-century Chinese altar table used as a sideboard. The table linens are of an eighteenth-century Portuguese colonial persuasion with their mixed Indian and Chinese echoes of the decorative motifs of Goa and Macao. Tiffany sterling silver Capstan saltshakers and pepper mills remind us of the New England seacoast's trade with the Far East.

The 1850s-style Bennington pottery poodles holding baskets of fruit in their mouths are giving a reasonably convincing imitation of domesticated English lions, but could probably more legitimately trace their ancestry to Ming celadon or Qianlong export-ware dogs.

The meal might include a bowl of "plum porridge," the soupy mixture of beef or lamb stewed in red wine with prunes, dried fruits and spices and thickened with bread crumbs that evolved over time into Christmas pudding. As the fruit and bread content increased, the meat was reduced to a bit of chopped suet, and brandy replaced the red wine.

AFTER *THE* NUTCRACKER

As New York children know, Christmas is incomplete without a
performance of Tchaikovsky's *Nutcracker* at the New York City Ballet.
There the sugar plums will dance and the tin soldiers will march just as they
have ever since George Balanchine introduced his version of *The
Nutcracker* to the delight of New York children both young and old in 1954.

When her daughters were still quite little, preeminent ballet enthusiast
and supporter Anne Bass arranged formal tea parties after the ballet that
perfectly satisfied a child's vision of old-fashioned Christmas. The tree was
garlanded with popcorn and cranberries, hung with candy canes and
gingerbread children, and tied with red satin bows. There would be teddy
bears and toy horses and circus wagons and fire engines for the little boys,
an ample contingent of exquisitely detailed dolls for the little girls, and,
naturally, an illustrated book of E. T. A. Hoffmann's Christmas tale *The
Nutcracker and the Mouse King* for each and every one.

Here at a Bass *Nutcracker* party, a twig basket filled with all-white
freesias, orchids, narcissus and double anemones centers the table set with
Tiffany "Biedermeier" faience, handpainted in the Austrian Tyrol with such
parties in mind. There are Christmas crackers and small enameled Tiffany
boxes filled with surprises, and there will be more than ample sugar plums
and other confections from Konfituerenburg too delicious to mention.

An antique hobbyhorse checks on last-minute details as the teddy bear
sits up to receive the guests. An octagonal Tiffany & Co. sterling silver tea
service announces that this is a very splendid event.

THE GLORIOUS TREE

"Decorating the Christmas tree was an annual ritual. There were the shiny old glass objects, carefully wrapped in tissue, that we brought up from the basement, the impossible tangle that was the many sets of colored lights, and the tinsel— the dreaded tinsel . . . Color and mixture of plain and intricate baubles were an important part of this festive equation, too."

— MARY TYLER MOORE,
After All, 1995

Whether they are peacocks with spun-glass tails and spring-clip feet, or Black Forest angels with white-spotted green wings, or jaunty toy soldiers, or tiny nativity scenes nestled in walnut shells, or maybe just mirrored-glass fruits and bells and trumpets—or better yet, if they are whole villages of miniature snow-roofed houses—the ornaments that find their way up from basements, down from attics and onto Christmas trees all speak their own strikingly vivid language of charmingly inconsequential symbolisms.

This odd discourse of images began long ago in the forests of Northern Europe when ancient Druids hung gilded apples on oak trees in celebration of the winter solstice while, unbeknownst to them, and far to the south, equally ancient Romans topped their Saturnalia trees with golden suns. Thereafter, all events leading to Christmas trees cavalierly abandoned order and logic to follow the arbitrary and meandering paths of fantasy.

The Druids' German descendants brought gingerbread men, gold-mesh bags of gilded chocolate coins, cinnamon star cookies and tinsel to the tree-trimming party. Then, in the mid-1860s, they added blown mirrored-glass ornaments and "icicles."

America contributed its own homemade touch with garlands of its native cranberries and popcorn, along with walnuts and pinecones.

Then, if all that wasn't enough, New England's Sarah Josepha Hale, tireless early champion of American Christmas and editor of that prodigy of nineteenth-century household how-to advice,

Godey's Lady's Book, proposed such novelties and eccentricities as the incorporation of ornamental pincushions for the ladies and decorative "pen wipers" for the men, which sound most unfestive today but must have found no small success among Victorians caught up in the relentless pursuit of ornamentalism.

In another, unrecorded moment of unbridled invention worthy of Sarah Hale, green mirrored-glass ornaments in the shape of cucumber pickles were created to be hidden in Christmas trees and later found by lucky children whose discoveries would not go unrewarded. Things having reached that point, it was anything goes that suited the season's fancy in trimmings.

Here, following an obstinate Yankee bent to the American imagination that places Christmas trees (even those typically German-American in their ornaments) among things English, a very English tree-trimming tea is served beside a partially trimmed Christmas tree decked out with quintessentially American cranberry and popcorn garlands and German gingerbread men, while awaiting its glass balls and colored lights.

The Charles X rosewood table with its appropriate-to-the-season neo-Gothic detailing is set with Tiffany gold-and-flower-spotted "Halcyon" bone china. The flat silver is naturally "English King," and the tea set and tray are all antique late-nineteenth-century Tiffany silver. There is a decanter of rum to spike the tea, and Tiffany sterling silver monkey candleholders illuminate the business at hand.

ADDRESSING CARDS AT LONGLEAT HOUSE

Begun in 1567, Longleat in Wiltshire was the first of what came to be known as Elizabethan England's "great prodigy" houses.

Here at a Georgian secretary desk whose neoclassic simplicity and monumental proportions echo the majestic scale and Renaissance flavor of Longleat House itself, cards are being addressed inviting guests to a Boxing Day luncheon.

A Tiffany "Honeycomb" sterling silver frame holds a family photo of Longleat's residents, the Marquess of Bath, his family and the family dog. There is an English cut-crystal decanter, also of stately proportion, reproduced from a prototype at Longleat for Tiffany's Stately Homes Crystal Collection, and the secretary's "tirettes" hold Tiffany candlesticks in pure eighteenth-century style. The small oil portrait of a well-fed eighteenth-century English nobleman, not a relative of the Marquess of Bath, is undoubtedly destined as a Christmas gift to a friend more in need of ancestors than the family of Longleat House.

In planning a Boxing Day luncheon, the wise will remember that on this very English holiday—when generosity of spirit reigns and gifts are boxed or reboxed and distributed to those more in need of favor than oneself—few guests this day after Christmas will be urgently in need of a copious repast. The inevitable excesses of Christmas are only hours behind, and light fare, which preferably will not include anything recycled from the Christmas table, is the desired order of the day.

In many English homes, both stately and less stately, kedgeree will be served. It is a festive, if easily made, dish of two parts poached smoked haddock, one part poached salmon, two parts long-grain rice cooked with some butter and a chopped onion and moistened and mixed together with a good portion of heavy cream and a bit of black pepper before being garnished with one quartered hard-boiled egg per person. To complete the mercifully light meal, there could be a salad of watercress, endive, walnuts and crumbled Roquefort; toasted French bread; and a dessert of poached spiced apples and pears.

> " *The only time I know of, in the long calendar of the year, when men and women seem by one consent to open their shut-up hearts freely, and to think of people below them as if they really were fellow-passengers . . .*'"
>
> —CHARLES DICKENS,
> *A Christmas Carol,* 1843

FINISHING TOUCHES

> *"As for me, my little brain*
> *Isn't very bright;*
> *Choose for me, old Santa Claus,*
> *What you think is right."*
>
> —ANONYMOUS,
> *Jolly Old St. Nicholas*

Before Clement Clarke Moore introduced St. Nick to the world in 1823 as a "right jolly old elf" "dressed in fur from his head to his foot" in that best-loved of all Christmas poems, *A Visit from St. Nicholas,* Santa had some years before been colorfully pictured by a lesser New York author, James Paulding, as a little pipe-smoking Dutchman more inspired by Peter Stuyvesant and New Amsterdam folklore than by the philanthropic patron of gifts, St. Nicholas of Myra. Paulding's St. Nick was attired in a navy blue pea jacket, red vest and yellow stockings, and accessorized with gold lace—old-world masculine finery that fashion experts today would at once identify as composed of the three out of the four most popular men's necktie pattern colors: blue, red and gold. Only green was missing to spell out "Christmas."

The colors of Christmas are the familiar and reassuring hues of men's ties, which are in turn traditional in both the Imari china used on, and the oriental carpets used under, Victorian Christmas dining tables. It is a hospitable color scheme of such fundamental solidity and staying power that any conforming Christmas decoration, no matter how contemporary, as in this so New York setting, asserts its authoritative and celebratory mood of solid homey tradition and old-fashioned period charm.

The red, green and gold of Christmas have their origins in every Western culture from the Romans' crown of green and red holly for the central figure at the December Saturnalia to the holly crowns worn by the Druids at their yule festivals.

In Northern Europe the red was also the color of Thor, the god of agriculture. Elsewhere it was the color of the fruits of the harvest past, of love and rebirth. The gold was for the gift of gold of the first mythical wise man, Gaspar, King of Tarsus; for St. Nicholas's attributes of three gold-coin-filled bags; and for the star announcing the Nativity.

The blue . . . well, the blue is a tradition added by Tiffany's, which has believed for over one hundred years that no Christmas is complete without Tiffany blue gift boxes under the tree and spilling from stockings.

Here at a late Christmas Eve supper, where the tree is most stylishly dressed in gold and surrounded by a veritable avalanche of red-bowed blue boxes, and where the highly designed stockings are filled but not yet hung, the senior family members will toast their handiwork from Tiffany "Rock Cut" champagne flutes, drink coffee from Tiffany cobalt-blue-and-platinum "Flags" Italian ceramic cups and eat a lemon-and-almond-flavored pound cake off of "Green Leaves" plates with "Palmette" flat silver.

Kate Greenaway in her *Language of Flowers* would have it that the variegated parrot tulips on the table symbolize "beautiful eyes" and the sunflower plate being gift-wrapped, "haughtiness." All of which could have led to Santa's placing a gold-headed cane by the fireplace to discourage haughtiness and vanity on Christmas.

There will be a moment to finish detailing the menu for the next evening's stylish Black-Tie Christmas Dinner.

THE GINGERBREAD PEOPLE'S LUNCH

"I make sketches and my friend cuts them out; lots of cats, fish too (because they're easy to draw), some apples, some watermelons, a few winged angels devised from saved-up sheets of Hershey bar tin foil. We use safety pins to attach these creations to the tree; as a final touch, we sprinkle the branches with shredded cotton (picked in August for this purpose)."

—TRUMAN CAPOTE,
A Christmas Memory, 1956

"Say what you will against children's fairy tales, you cannot deny that we fall in love with them as children, and that they have become part of our psyche," observed a critic named Hermann Laroche reviewing Tchaikovsky's 1892 ballet *The Nutcracker*.

Fairy tales, too, are undeniably a part of Christmas celebrations, when everything from gingerbread to nutcrackers assumes human qualities and joins in the festivities.

The theme with the maximum possibilities for fairy tales is, naturally, love—its adventures, its adversities and its eventual triumph, where the rats and mice have been vanquished and the prince and princess adjourn to the kingdom of toys and candies. There they are married beside a river of milk with shores of pudding before going off in a most Christmasy sleigh hitched to reindeer; or, at least, that is how it all turns out in *The Nutcracker*.

The story will be familiar to the grown-up children at this holiday luncheon and probably to the gingerbread men as well, who will all recognize the candy cane among the sweets on the roof of the lavishly frosted gingerbread house as a sign that Bouffon, the candy cane from Tchaikovsky's ballet, may dance in at any moment.

Although the gifts that come to life as the characters of Hans Christian Andersen's *The Hardy Tin Soldier* are exchanged on a different kind of birthday—and the house is not gingerbread but a cardboard castle, and the enemy is a water rat rather than the Mouse King—the Tin Soldier on the Christmas tree will remind the guests that all fairy tales do not end alike. The Tin Soldier and his love, the cardboard dancer with the narrow blue neck ribbon and the tinsel rose, both end up in the stove, and all that is left is a lump of tin in the shape of a heart.

The hearts on this table's Tiffany heart beaker are not tin but sterling silver, as are the "Audubon" spoons, unlike the "old tin spoon" that parented the hardy little soldier and his twenty-four brothers. Nor is there a tin drum, but there is a Tiffany sterling silver drum salt seller.

A traditional Tiffany pet, "Rover, the Traveling Dog," lies on his suitcase and observes the goings-on from the white marble mantelpiece.

An Amish quilt covers the lunch table, and a nineteenth-century American cow weathervane inspects the table setting, where each guest will receive a bird-shaped Tiffany porcelain box to play any role in Christmas tales the heart desires.

There is a decanter of chilled white wine to accompany the "great fish" who "snapped up" the Tin Soldier and who is being transformed in the kitchen by the cook into delicious *quenelles de brochet*.

As so much here is in the world of make-believe, so is the Christmas tree, which was painted for the occasion on a cut-out wooden panel by New York artist Katharine Barnwell. Its toy soldier, its red satin bows, its bears and rabbits and cherubs, its bluebirds and its painted toy drum and brass horn, as well as its candy canes, are all only as real as the kingdom of toys and sweets upon whose Christmas pudding shores such Christmas trees grow.

RED, WHITE AND RED

Christmas red: it imparts a warm and healthy glow to the faces of guests at the table and an air of excitement so fitting to the festal season. Since 1931, when the artist-illustrator Haddon Sundblom was commissioned by Coca-Cola to modernize and redesign Santa Claus, taking him out of furs and dressing him all in Christmas red with snow-white trim, it has remained the primary fashion color of the season.

The legendary American high priestess of fashion, Diana Vreeland, decorated the living room of her Park Avenue apartment completely in red to bask in the flattering glow of Christmas's color the year through, and there her guests basked in the glow of her quixotic, generously proportioned spirit, which was at every moment prepared to give Santa Claus a run for his bag of tricks—or, at least,

formidable competition for center stage.

Here in a theatrical setting worthy of Mrs. Vreeland, there are not one but two Christmas trees placed in true high-priestess style on either side of the fireplace. Both are hung entirely with Tiffany silver ornaments and accessorized with fat red bows. Two giant Tiffany "Christmas Tree" Venetian glass candlesticks stand in for altar candles on the mantel. The tablecloth, service plates and candles are all Christmas red, as is the Tiffany "Corail" chinoiserie

urn holding red, white and pink roses at the center of the festivities. There are also adequate notes of gold.

"Yes, Virginia, there is a Santa Claus. He exists as certainly as love and generosity and devotion exist . . ."

—FRANCIS P. CHURCH,
New York Sun, editorial, September 21, 1897

HOME FOR THE HOLIDAYS

> *"On the table a snow-white cloth was spread; upon it stood a shining dinner service; the roast goose smoked gloriously, stuffed with apples and dried plums."*
>
> —HANS CHRISTIAN ANDERSEN,
> *The Little Match Girl,* 1848

The image of American Christmas is a late-nineteenth-century image of Currier & Ives–type genre scenes, of country life in a villagescape of snow and pine trees, Colonial Georgian frame houses and white-painted Christopher Wren–like steepled churches. There is an air of busied activity, with the roads animated by horses, and sleighs, and children and dogs, and men bringing in wood for the fire. There are invariably hills in the background and a red barn or two and maybe a stone fence punctuating the expanses of snow, and once in a while there is even a mill. The studied naïveté of high folk art is essential to the persuasive charm of such images, which have flourished on American Christmas and seasonal greeting cards for more than a century.

With all due respect to Messrs. Currier & Ives, the most remarkable practitioner of the genre and the most popular American folk artist of this century was Anna Mary Robertson ("Grandma") Moses, who only began painting scenes she recalled from her nineteenth-century American childhood while in her seventies. For two decades she produced numerous works celebrating American rural traditions, community life and the honest and heartfelt "There's no place like home" feelings that Christmas and the holidays inspire.

Here under the French Art Deco Daum crystal chandelier of an insistently urban and urbane dining room, the table is set for a holiday dinner. A splendid Grandma Moses painting, *Over the River to Grandma's,* hangs above the fireplace. The river and the woods and the mill with its mill wheel iced over and stopped for the winter are all there, and a dog is running to greet the family members returning home for the holidays in a sleigh drawn by two horses.

In contrast to Grandma Moses' painting, the room's tree exhibits a more worldly and sophisticated view of the holidays with its stylish combination of double ribbon bows and glittering gold paper poinsettias and roses.

A centerpiece of laurel leaves, although they have no verifiable Christmas symbolism, maintains an air of triumphant celebration that nicely carries on the graceful neoclassic dignity of the Art Deco fireplace's fluted marble columns and the architectural detailing of the Russian neoclassic chairs.

The white-damask-clothed table is set with Tiffany's versatile "Holiday" bone china in red, green and gold. The Art Deco theme is encouraged by Tiffany's "Century" flat silver, designed in 1937 to commemorate the company's one hundredth year.

The fanciful red-and-green Tiffany trompe-l'oeil Italian soup tureen is in the form of an impressively large bunch of radishes topped by an artichoke and might contain a cream of artichoke soup or a ragout of artichokes and lobster.

Three red, clear and blue double "Baluster" Venetian glass candlesticks from Tiffany's "Festivity" collection by Archimede Seguso illuminate the mantelpiece.

The menu for the Christmas Night Dinner, which follows, is from a collection of menus, both realistic and unrealistic, gathered by twentieth-century America's best-loved hostess, Jacqueline Kennedy Onassis. It is from Florence Pritchett Smith's 1966 book, *These Entertaining People,* from which Mrs. Onassis planned meals for the Onassis yacht.

Over the River to Grandma's by Grandma Moses. Copyright © 1996, Grandma Moses Properties Co., New York.

CHRISTMAS NIGHT DINNER

LOBSTER À L'AMÉRICAINE
RICE PILAF

ROAST PHEASANT
(ON A PLATTER COVERED WITH FRIED BREAD)
ROAST HAM, CUMBERLAND SAUCE
MOUSSE OF WILD DUCK MADE WITH FOIE GRAS
COLD POACHED CHICKEN WITH MOUSSE OF FOIE GRAS,
CHAUD-FROID SAUCE
SMALL ROAST STUFFED TURKEY
GALANTINE OF CHICKEN

ROAST SADDLE OF LAMB, MINT SAUCE
PÂTÉ OF SQUAB IN A PASTRY CRUST
PÂTÉ OF HARE IN A TERRINE
ROAST SQUAB WITH FOIE GRAS AND TRUFFLES
PÂTÉ DE FOIE GRAS

MIXED VEGETABLE SALAD, MAYONNAISE DRESSING
SALAD MARGUERITE
(A WINTER SALAD CONTAINING CAULIFLOWER, POTATOES,
FRENCH BEANS, ASPARAGUS TIPS, ALL MARINATED AND
COVERED WITH MAYONNAISE, AND DECORATED WITH
HARD-BOILED EGGS CUT IN THE SHAPE OF DAISIES)
MIXED GREEN SALAD

GLACE IMPÉRIALE
(A BOMBE MOLD LINED WITH MANDARINE
IMPÉRIALE—FLAVORED ICE CREAM
AND THE CENTER FILLED WITH FRESH RASPBERRY ICE)
PLATTER OF LITTLE FANCY CAKES
BÛCHE DE NOËL

CHAMPAGNE

THE DINNER DANCE

*"I believe in Santa Claus . . . and in others too generous
and too rich to mention."*

—SUZY (AILEEN MEHLE), 1996

Throughout the 1960s, '70s and into the '80s, glittering Tiffany Christmas supper dances were held in the Edwardian splendor of the Versailles Suite at Fifth Avenue's grand St. Regis Hotel. These biennial highlights of the New York social season were hosted by Louis Comfort Tiffany's great-grandson Henry B. Platt, who invited the one hundred most beautiful women in international society. It was up to them to choose a suitable escort who, needless to say, would have to be given Tiffany's stamp of approval.

The members of this most select club of socialites, movie stars, peeresses, celebrated beauties and their well-heeled escorts would all be photographed making their entrances to the ball in a setting of ultimate Tiffany style and luxury while the queen of society columnists, "Suzy," would note the antics of each, including those "too beautiful, too stylish and too titled to mention."

Here at the entry to the 1982 party in a décor of richly carved Indian screens and furniture upholstered and draped in party-minded gold and silver paisleys, the table is set with Tiffany "Audubon" vermeil flat silver and "Bamboo" vermeil candlesticks. Tiffany "Nuit de Chine" porcelain boxes hold Christmas candies, and one of the guests, obviously too privileged and too jeweled to mention, has discarded her Paloma Picasso Tiffany necklace of gold, imperial topaz, diamonds and pearls on her butter plate.

H.R.H. Princess Chantal of France's Christmas Supper

Following in the footsteps of her great-great-grandfather King Louis Philippe of France, who visited America as the twenty-four-year-old Duke of Orléans in 1796, Princess Chantal of France came to spend several years of the 1980s with her family in a small turn-of-the-century house near New York. There she received her new American friends in the noblest and most hospitable fashion, surrounded by souvenirs of her very French and very, very noble family.

Her table for a formal Christmas supper is set with Tiffany "Chrysanthemum" vermeil flat silver, as well as with a Louis XV–style vermeil centerpiece tureen and a dazzling array of other Tiffany vermeil silver. Four vases of shocking pink orchids give a Parisian touch and hint at rich purple associations with royalty.

The place card in the foreground is for the princess's sister-in-law, the Duchess of Orléans, and that next to it is for her husband, the Baron François-Xavier of Sambucy.

A portrait of Louis Philippe temporarily borrowed from the Orléans family's Château d'Eu in Normandy looks on from the background, where the princess's three children, Axel, Alexandre and Kildine, hope that one of their mother's indescribably delicious flourless chocolate cakes will also be waiting, possibly, if all are lucky, accompanied by a bowl of her equally delicious dark chocolate mousse.

"Fine old Christmas with the snowy hair and ruddy face had done his duty that year in the noblest fashion, and had set off his rich gifts of warmth and colour with all the heightening contrast of frost and snow."

— GEORGE ELIOT, *The Mill on the Floss*, 1860

A NOT SO FRUGAL
CHRISTMAS EVE REPAST

"'Say "Merry Christmas!"... and let's be happy. You don't know what a nice—what a beautiful, nice gift I've got for you'"

—O. HENRY,
The Gift of the Magi, 1906

New York's *Commercial Advertiser* of Sunday afternoon, December 15, 1873, advised its readers that whether they "buy or not, it will pay them to take a ramble over to Tiffany's palatial store, which will be open evenings during the holidays."

There they would find gifts befitting the splendor of this setting for a family Christmas Eve. The Tiffany "English King" flat silver and "Corinthïan Column" candlesticks, along with the topiary tree of dried roses by New York designer Valorie Hart and the regal porcelain swan (who is, as is his nature, "swaning about" by the rose tree), all suggest that the gift in the blue box will be as glorious as was in Santa Claus's power to buy.

The *Advertiser*'s value-conscious reporter made his own suggestions for Christmas 1873, which hold good today:

What a grand display of dazzling splendors, and what a sumptuous mental festival is daily and nightly enjoyed by the refined and artistic who throng Tiffany & Co.'s palace of gems.

Arithmetic stands aghast at a mere contemplation of the number and variety of beautiful souvenirs.

Every sort of rare gem and curious metal [is] here manufactured and artistically manipulated into a multitude of *recherché* forms, both useful and ornamental. Diamond crosses of all sizes, sending forth a thousand prismatic hues. The queenly solitaire, so grandly gorgeous, possessing such an undisputed worth, would make a lovely Christmas gift for Monsieur to present to his betrothed.

A pretty cluster-ring is a valuable gift. An emerald surrounded with tiny diamonds forms a very handsome ring, one *apropos* for a fond mother to surprise her beloved daughter with a holiday keepsake. Another pretty style of ring, a clear white pearl, resting in the center of a circle of rare diamonds. A handsome seal ring for your darling Edward, or one of those lovely amethyst rings would also make a pretty token of love.

Gifts exchanged by dear relatives and fond lovers should be as costly as possible. The most appropriate expression of love and true affection is some ornament that may be cherished in tender remembrance of the donor.

A dear brother anxious to please his sister, and also desirous of laying out his money in the purchase of some gift that can be kept for years, would do well to look at those lovely pearl sets. There is a pure, sensitive beauty to be found in pearls, that does not appear in any other precious stones. A gold ring, with one large pearl, is unique and chastely beautiful. A cluster-ring never fails to please the artistic eye.

A full set of pearls makes a valuable and quietly elegant bridal gift to friends or relatives who will enter into the state of matrimony on Christmas Day.

Those seeking small souvenirs will find something to suit them in the line of trinkets, such as charms for the watch chain, either for gentlemen or ladies. Tiffany has a large assortment of these cunning Christmas gifts: The designs of some are exceedingly novel, and the workmanship of all is par excellence.

SANTA BABY

Carol Lawrence, who later starred in *West Side Story,* was in the cast of Leonard
Sillman's *New Faces of 1952;* however, when Eartha Kitt stalked onto the stage of the
Royale Theater on the evening of Friday, May 15, 1952, and sang *Monotonous,* there
was just one new star on Broadway.

"Eartha Kitt not only looks incendiary but she can make a song burst into
flames," raved Brooks Atkinson.

Famed artist-designer Raoul Pène du Bois had given Miss Kitt a bare stage
furnished with three satin-covered chaise longues, and costume designer Thomas
Becher had clad her in basic black satin men's pajamas. Arthur Siegel had provided
music only Eartha Kitt could turn into a sensation, and June Carroll had added lyrics
that anyone who heard remembers to this day. Miss Kitt knew what to do with all of it.
The remarkable young American dancer-singer from Columbia, South Carolina, who
had previously been cast as Helen of Troy in Orson Welles's production of
Christopher Marlowe's *Doctor Faustus,* intoned, "For what it's worth, throughout the
earth, I'm known as femme fatale"; and forever after, that has been her image.

In 1952 alleged admirers in *Monotonous* had, to no avail, offered her the Black Sea
for her "swimming pool" and then the Taj Mahal, which she "sent back." By the next
year, 1953, Joan Javits, Phil Springer and Tony Springer had written *Santa Baby.* That
song became Eartha Kitt's possibly best-loved hit.

There she was, at it again with materialistic purrings to Santa for a Christmas list
of sables, diamonds, a duplex and a light blue convertible, along with a generous
bonus of Christmas checks. Here Miss Kitt awaits Santa's anticipated visit, and he
will appear, since who could refuse her such modest requests.

The three chaises are all upholstered in chartreuse satin, Miss Kitt's well-thought-
out variation on Christmas green. Santa has sent ahead a large bouquet of Christmas
red roses, to which Miss Kitt has, to stave off monotony, added a few pink orchids
(probably from one more man "who looked like Montgomery Clift"), and the black
satin pajamas are laid out to be donned as soon as yet another unnamed admirer can
be gotten off the phone.

Eartha Kitt and Santa Baby will dine off gadroon-edged Tiffany sterling silver
trays set with "American Garden" flat silver and Tiffany "Black Shoulder"
handpainted French porcelain, which may remind Miss Kitt of early days singing in
Paris cabarets, where she was "discovered" by Leonard Sillman.

AN OLD FAMILIAR CHRISTMAS

The polished red apples and clove-studded oranges centering this high-Victorian-style holiday table promote the earthy, deep-rooted vitality that marks traditional Christmas festivities.

Decked out with gold ribbon bows and sitting on a silver leaf plate reproduced by Tiffany & Co. from an eighteenth-century original at Chatsworth in England, they complement the richly ornamented Tiffany china used on the table. Orange-red and gold, chinoiserie-patterned "Corail" covered bowls sit on "Halcyon" dinnerware, whose animated pink and yellow florets, Tiffany blue ribbons and gold-spotted cobalt-blue background all announce a very special family dinner.

A Christmas-red-and-cobalt-blue-striped damask tablecover unifies the intricate table furnishings, while in the mid-nineteenth-century English painting a King Charles spaniel held by a contented Victorian child wearing a chaste white party dress seems eager to participate in any or all of the evening's many delights.

The high chair for the youngest member of the household is filled with antique building blocks, a new silver baby cup and a blue box tied with a red ribbon; and to be sure that no young desire is unfulfilled, several antique American toy horses on the mantle await the arrival of the infant focus of the evening's revelries.

A MERRY DINNER

Like many good Northern European legends, Santa Claus spent much of his early career riding about on a white horse or pony. That was until 1821, when New York's *The Children's Friend* included a verse referring to Santa as the proud possessor of a sleigh and reindeer, so paving the way for Clement C. Moore in 1823 to introduce the world to eight reindeer on a first-name basis in *A Visit from St. Nicholas*. Since then, deer of all kinds have been an integral part of Christmas.

Here a nineteenth-century Japanese bronze cousin of Cupid or Blitzen stands by the as yet unornamented tree on Christmas Eve. Presents are being wrapped and rewrapped, as is so often the case. A wastebasket to take care of used ribbons and tissue paper has been tastefully covered with a hollyhock-patterned wallpaper to match the chintz upholstery on the Sheraton chinoiserie chairs.

The red satin Christmas ribbons have inspired a red satin upholstered armchair, where some happy member of the family can collapse, wrapped up in the setting's hollyhock-chintz-lined faux-fur throw, and enjoy a last glass of cognac after the tree is decorated and all the gifts are under its branches.

The buffet table is set with Tiffany "Chrysanthemum" silver, a participant in Christmas celebrations since 1880, and "Marina" handpainted Italian ceramic dinnerware, whose green leaves and red flowers carry along the evening's theme.

> *"All the stockings you will find*
> *hanging in a row:*
> *Mine will be the shortest one,*
> *You'll be sure to know."*
>
> —ANONYMOUS,
> *Jolly Old St. Nicholas*

CHRISTMAS HAS COME!

Everyone is on sure ground at Christmas when, surrounded by the time-honored trappings of the holidays, an unself-conscious spirit of openness and generosity flourishes.

Red-and-green wool socks hang by the fire, and are filled to overflowing with small Tiffany gift boxes and red-and-white-striped sugar canes that all collaborate to get the mood off to a running start. A Bavarian rococo mirror carved with a flock of musician cupids, hanging as if in flight above the mantle, does nothing to discourage thoughts of Christmas carols. Pine and pinecones are, of course, a necessity; and if there are stuffed animals, at least one dog and a few books of children's stories, the atmosphere will be the better for it.

Every needed trapping of Christmas is here in abundance for this breakfast to please children not able to wait a minute past nine for their gifts.

The stockings hang on a fine George III wood mantle carved in the 1780s, and the breakfast table is set with Tiffany "Shell and Thread" silver and "Napoleon Ivy" china, first made by Wedgwood for the exiled Emperor Napoleon's use at Longwood House on the southern Atlantic island of St. Helena, where, beginning in 1815, he spent six Christmases.

WOBURN ABBEY GALA DINNER

> *"The tree . . . was brilliantly lighted by a multitude of little tapers; and everywhere sparkled and glittered with bright objects."*
>
> —CHARLES DICKENS,
> *A Christmas Tree*, 1850

One of England's most celebrated and most visited stately homes, Woburn Abbey began its career as a Cistercian monastery in the twelfth century. The monastery was dissolved in the 1530s and the property given by King Edward VI to his Lord Privy Seal, John Russell, in 1549. Since then, the Russells have risen to become the Dukes of Bedford, and the abbey was rebuilt by the Palladian architect Henry Flitcroft, working for the 4th Duke in the 1740s.

The 4th Duke of Bedford's fondness for the Palladian style in architecture, fortunately for the Russell family, extended to a passion for the architectural and cityscape paintings of his contemporary, the great Venetian painter Antonio Canal, called "Canaletto." Through the agency of Canaletto's principal dealer in Venice, Joseph Smith, who was conveniently also the English consul, the 4th Duke acquired twenty-two views of Venice and two larger festival subjects for the extremely modest sum of £188.

This unequaled collection of Canaletto's work was noted in a 1771 inventory of Bedford House in London as being divided between the "Little Eating Room" and the "Large Dining Room." The majority of them now hang in the dining room of Woburn Abbey, where they were no doubt placed around 1790 by Henry Holland, who redecorated Woburn's dining room in a rather chaste Louis XVI style for the 5th Duke.

Here the Most Honourable Marquess of Tavistock, the son of the present Duke of Bedford, entertains at a gala holiday dinner in a lesser "eating room."

The Georgian-style table, surrounded by magnificently detailed dining chairs (from the Baker Furniture Stately Homes Collection), is set, in keeping with the gold theme of Woburn's dining room, with a glittering display of Tiffany & Co. vermeil sterling silver, including "Hampton" flatware, four-branch candelabra and a whimsical centerpiece in the form of an English Regency chinoiserie pagoda birdcage.

An ornamental garden statue of a life-sized stag has tipped his antlers with golden Christmas tree balls and come in from the park, possibly to keep out of the way of Woburn's famous lions, which are the delight of visitors to the abbey, but may not be the delight of the local deer.

Dinner will begin with a spinach soufflé, followed by a fresh tomato consommé and after that poached salmon with hollandaise sauce (which was not named after Woburn's interior decorator Henry Holland).

The main course will be baked ham with hot Cumberland sauce, that great traditional English accompaniment to salted and smoked meats which is made with red currant jelly and port wine and flavored with much dry mustard and lesser amounts of grated orange and lemon rind, ground cloves and ginger, brown sugar and cayenne pepper. It is thickened with cornstarch and can have golden or black raisins and slivered almonds as well as a bit of orange juice added.

The ham will be served with broad beans and potatoes *à la dauphinoise*. There will be a black currant sorbet for dessert, served in a covered porcelain artichoke with bird finials based on models made at Chelsea in London in the mid-1750s.

Christmas Dinner 1986
Woburn Abbey
The Most Honourable Marquess of Tavistock

Spinach Soufflé
with Anchovy Butter

Fresh Tomato Consommé Soup

Poached Salmon Hollandaise

Steamed Broccoli   Rice

Cucumber and Dill

Hot Baked Ham
with Cumberland Sauce

Broad Beans   Potatoes Dauphinoise

Blackcurrant Sorbet

Devils on Horseback

Christmas Dinner 1986
Woburn Abbey
The Most Honourable Marquess of Tavistock

Spinach Soufflé
with Anchovy Butter

Fresh Tomato Consommé Soup

Poached Salmon Hollandaise
Steamed Broccoli   Rice
Cucumber and Dill

Hot Baked Ham
with Cumberland Sauce
Broad Beans   Potatoes Dauphinoise

Blackcurrant Sorbet

Devils on Horseback

DINNER IN THE CUBHOUSE

> *"Notwithstanding their Mother's deep
> conviction, the cubs were not remarkably big
> or bright; yet they were a remarkable family."*
>
> —ERNEST THOMPSON SETON,
> *The Biography of a Grizzly*, 1900

Teddy bears have been an absolute necessity in every child's, and in a fair number of adults', lives and Christmases ever since Richard Steiff first designed them in 1903 to honor President Theodore ("Teddy") Roosevelt.

Thanks to A. A. Milne, "Teddys" were soon joined by the "Pooh" bears that proliferated after Milne's much-loved children's books *Winnie-the-Pooh* and *The House at Pooh Corner* appeared in the 1920s.

Pooh and Teddy arrived in modern times to join such venerable members of the Bear Hall of Fame as Robert Southey's Great, Huge Bear, Middle-Sized Bear and Little, Small, Wee Bear from his *Story of the Three Bears*—who had all three made their debut in bear history in 1834. Then, of course, there was Paddington Bear.

Here one bear cub has already arrived at a children's dinner and appropriated one of the guests' presents, which seems only fair considering the rather selfish human behavior patterns exposed in the *Story of the Three Bears*.

The children and bears could have a lively discussion on preferences for Southey's original version of that story or for the sentimentalized Victorian version in which "a pretty child, with bright yellow hair that shone and glittered in the sun like gold" replaced "the little old woman" with an "ugly, dirty head" of Southey's story.

The bear cubs and the more spirited children will all argue that Southey's ending to the tale is by far the more witty, to say nothing of Southey's literary superiority:

Out the little old woman jumped; and whether she broke her neck in the fall; or ran into the wood and was lost there; or found her way out of the wood, and was taken up by the constable and sent to the House of Correction for a vagrant as she was, I cannot tell. But the Three Bears never saw anything more of her.

The more sensitive children and smallest bears may, however, prefer the sweeter Victorian ending:

[Goldilocks] fell plump on the ground, and had to sit still for a few moments to find out where she was. But it seemed as if the woods were full of bears, and so she kept on running as hard as ever she could until she was well out of the forest, and in sight of her own home.

Oh, what joy it was to be safe inside her own home! And Goldilocks made up her mind never again to enter anyone's house without being invited, and never to make herself quite so much at home as she did in the bears' house.

The covered porridge pots, as well as the plates and bear house candlesticks on the party table, are all Tiffany "Biedermeier" Austrian faience. The Christmas red napkins are decorated with Tiffany silver candy cane ornaments tied with green satin ribbon bows. The table is animated by colorfully enameled silver clowns, acrobats and animals from Tiffany's "Gene Moore Circus," designed by Tiffany's longtime resident wizard of window display, who understood so clearly the workings of the hearts and minds of children and bears, and who would advise all the guests at the party to "Bear and Forbear."

THE CHRISTMAS CAKE

"Too composed and sedate . . . I wanted more abandon . . . and joyous expression," said His Grace the 6th Duke of Devonshire in 1832 as he contemplated the great gold-and-white dining room at Chatsworth, just decorated for him by Sir Jeffry Wyatville.

His comment must have amused almost everyone, as there was nothing in the least bit sedate about the room's barely clothed, but larger than life-sized, marble bacchantes flanking the fireplaces, nor about the great gold-masked and whorling-legged, garlanded Kent-style sideboard holding an awesome display of the most elaborate Paul Storr silver, including two monumental candelabra, each sporting three shepherd boys playing their pipes under silver palm trees, which were crowned by ten-branched candleholders, the whole production supported by recumbent deer.

The hall's coffered and gently vaulted ceiling caused the 6th Duke to remark that to be in Chatsworth's dining room was "like dining in a great trunk, and you expect the lid to open."

His first guest in this splendid new décor was a thirteen-year-old princess, who five years later, in 1837, went on to become that model of sedateness, Queen Victoria. She may or may not have been amused by the Duke's comments; however, it is unlikely that she shared his desire for "more abandon" or that she found the bacchantes too sedate.

She would, no doubt, have been amused by the neo-Gothic Christmas cake in this totally joyous setting for the current Duke and Duchess of Devonshire.

A. W. N. Pugin himself, who neo-Gothicized everything he touched during Victoria's reign, including and not least the Houses of Parliament, could not have designed a more splendid and whimsically neo-Gothic cake than this, made for the occasion by New York's Colette Peters.

Punch will be served out of a massive silver monteith bowl, and there are assorted cookies on a very grand silver leaf tray made after one at Chatsworth, as is the silver cake plate, for Tiffany's Stately Homes Silver Collection.

An antique Wedgwood black basalt bust of Paris judges the setting and awards it a Tiffany vermeil rose for "joyous expression."

If the guests are fortunate, the Duchess of Devonshire may offer them a small glass of her favorite sloe gin as a holiday treat.

THE LIBRARY SUPPER

Not to be outdone by the flamboyant red macaw on the library's lavishly flowered Victorian folding screen, the Tiffany silver pheasant perched in the so-very-grand Regency bookcase wears a red silk ribbon bow around his neck in celebration of Christmas Eve.

The conservatively literary family dining table is set with "Tiffany Garland" bone china, which sports its own red ribbon, and "King William" silver, named for the none-too-literary King William III, who nonetheless gave his name to a couple of celebrated American towns and educational institutions.

At each place, there are Tiffany magnifying glasses sitting on the leopard print napkins and two Tiffany English enameled copper "Santa" boxes holding salt and pepper.

Tiffany silver pagoda candlesticks designed in the late 1950s by Tiffany's then design director, Van Day Truex, center the table with English Regency–style flair. The table ornaments include a cheery, if demure, bouquet of pointy little miniature white tulips, contrasting stylishly with the floral eruptions of the library's painted screen.

Three finely bound books of a seemingly most serious nature have been exchanged among family members. They will be added to the library's collection, and after dinner, passages will be read from each to amuse everyone.

From the volume on Disraeli, there will be insights into the intricacies, not of Victorian Christmases but certainly of Victorian politics.

There will not be time to open the third volume quite simply because the second, James Anthony Froude's *History of England from the Fall of Wolsey to the Defeat of the Spanish Armada*, published in 1875, contains ample anecdote and adventure for any one evening's readings.

Here in Volume IV, which dispatches no less a personage than Henry VIII shortly after the Christmas of 1546 and then begins investigations of the unfortunate Edward VI, there are such intriguing headings as "Seymour Desires to Marry Elizabeth," "Spread of Wild Opinions," "The German Princes Offer Their Services to England," "Female Intrigues in Paris," "Seymour Is Arrested," "Loss of the 'Mary Rose,' " and all ending in a flourish with "War in Italy."

If the attention of the family had strayed during accounts of the intrigues of the Queen of Navarre and Madame d'Étampes at the intrigue-frenzied court of Francis I in Paris, they would, no doubt, have been amused by the less literary account of the "easy, timid and self-indulgent" Cardinal del Monte, who, on ascending to the papal throne in 1550 as Julius III, bestowed his "red hat and the high dignity of a cardinal on a favorite and beautiful page who had the care of his Holiness's monkey."

The red macaw has had the chance to observe during the course of the evening that the bestowing of red-ribboned Tiffany blue boxes on relations meets with invariable success, whereas the strange habit of bestowing red hats on pages who attend to monkey business might be met with less general enthusiasm.

CHRISTMAS MORNING WITH WASHINGTON IRVING

Although Washington Irving's tale of *Rip Van Winkle* and his *Legend of Sleepy Hollow* are better known, Irving's account of Christmas circa 1820 at Squire Bracebridge's mansion deserves honor in the literature of Christmas. Filled with charming description of rural games and customs, it evokes

the "home-bred, social and joyous" mood of an old Christmas.

"Now," admonished the Christmas-spirited Irving, "plums and spice, sugar and honey square it among pies and broth. Now or never must music be in tune, for the youth must dance and sing to get

them a heat, while the aged sit by the fire."

Here Mrs. Peter C. Rockefeller designs a setting evocative of Christmases at the author's famed Hudson River home, Sunnyside. From a Tiffany silver frame, Irving supervises the revelry. The table set with Tiffany "Ivy" dishes recalls Irving's fondness for ivy as it "winds its rich foliage about the Gothic arch."

And a proud Tiffany silver Christmas stag sits on books by Irving in front of the neo-Gothic windows.

"[Christmas] is calling back the children of a family . . . to assemble about the paternal hearth . . . there to grow young and loving again among the endearing mementoes of childhood."

—WASHINGTON IRVING,
The Sketch Book of Geoffrey Crayon, Gent., 1819–20

> *"And as they went it became beautiful spring, with green and with flowers."*
>
> —HANS CHRISTIAN ANDERSEN,
> *The Snow Queen,* 1846

HAPPY BE THE HOLIDAY!

Russia's kindly patron St. Nicholas, in saintly fashion, tossed bags of gold coins through a poor nobleman's window so that his three daughters might have dowries and be married.

Evoking St. Nicholas and other things Russian, here Mrs. John Gutfreund breakfasts on fresh beluga malossol caviar served with sour cream and boiled potatoes, while a festive little red bag of Tiffany gift coins has been tossed next to a small pine tree jauntily ornamented with little Tiffany woven silver baskets of fresh flowers.

An eighteenth-century silver bust of Russia's Catherine the Great, who earlier in life as Princess of Anhalt-Zerbst had no need of St. Nick providing her with a dowry, looks on.

Mrs. Gutfreund's 1880s American brass bed is hung with antique laces from Alençon, Lille, Chantilly, and Coggeshall—along with a yard or two from Carrickmacross for good measure.

Breakfast tea will be served Russian-style in crystal mugs and stirred with Tiffany silver spoons in the Renaissance Revival pattern "San Lorenzo," introduced in Russia's last imperial year, 1916.

SANTA WAS HERE

The rag rugs are littered with a veritable avalanche of Tiffany boxes; the stockings are hung by the chimney and filled to bursting; cinnamon sticks and lady apples tied with red ribbons, sugar canes and gingerbread men have taken up positions on the tree; and a stuffed bear appropriates the nineteenth-century Orkney chair left for Santa to enjoy the cognac, stollen and coffee set out by the fire on a maple milking stool.

Bright red poinsettias play their old familiar role, and everything echoes the old-fashioned and heartwarming New England country mood of the snowy landscape painting, *Out for Christmas Trees,* by everyone's favorite painter of rural Christmas charm, Anna Mary Robertson ("Grandma") Moses.

There is a fine dappled antique hobbyhorse to brighten the spirits of the older children, as well as a lovable carousel-inspired rocking-horse chair for the babies, and Santa's bag still contains a few more serious Tiffany presents for the grown-ups.

The children will arrive in the nursery at any moment. Then the remaining dolls and toys can come out of their boxes and assure all assembled that the spirit of Christmas has taken charge of the long, wintery season, and in every corner of the room there will be a mood of well-being approaching euphoria.

Out for the Christmas Trees by Grandma Moses. Copyright © 1996, Grandma Moses Properties Co., New York.

CHRISTMAS BREAKFAST AT LENNOXLOVE CASTLE

The at once romantic and solid Lennoxlove Castle of the Dukes of Hamilton started off as a fourteenth-century Scottish fortress. Thanks to a Hamilton Earl of Arran, who was Regent for Mary Queen of Scots, it boasts souvenirs of that ill-fated lady, among them a magnificent fifteenth-century silver jewel casket given to her by her first husband, Francis II of France, possibly to house the famed Hanoverian Pearls, a gift from her mother-in-law, Catherine de' Medici.

Since 1946, Lennoxlove has been the official home of the Dukes of Hamilton and Brandon and now houses the treasures of art and furnishings that once adorned Hamilton Palace, which was, until it was demolished in 1919, the largest private house in Britain.

At this Christmas breakfast given by the 15th Duke, there will be a lively discussion of His Grace's pet, bright red "Nomad," which he developed and built. A picture of the Nomad parked in front of Lennoxlove Castle can be viewed on the architect's table beside the buffet. The Duke, who has a fondness for racing cars as well as for agricultural vehicles, describes it as "strong, lasting, economic and practical—and, if you want, luxurious."

The breakfast buffet is furnished with Tiffany "Yellow Flowers" plates and "English King" silver and ornamented by a Venetian glass "Sweetmeat Tree," an impractical and luxurious Tiffany classic since the 1950s.

THE CHILDREN'S CHRISTMAS

Whether the Tiffany porcelain parrot candlesticks on this Christmas Eve dinner table are "Poor Robin Crusoe," as Ebenezer Scrooge exclaimed to the childlike Ghost of Christmas Past, or "Iago," or "Polly" (who might want one of the Christmas crackers), or whether they are related to the birds on the "Audubon" flat silver, makes very little difference to the vivid imaginations of children on Christmas Eve, when all is fairy tale and storybook,

when men are made out of gingerbread and ribbons out of spun sugar, and when Paddington Bear might arrive to dine at any moment.

Whether the Tiffany "Trompe l'Oeil" ceramic apples that decorate the table center are symbolic of Eden, or whether they descend from the ornaments of winter festival "paradise trees" of medieval times, will never make them as greatly appealing to children as their porcelain apple box counterparts,

which the children know to contain sweets yet more delectable and sticky than those already visible on the table.

And whether Tom Smith, the London confectioner, invented the Christmas cracker in 1840 while admiring bonbon wrappings in Paris, or whether Tiffany's made the red, green and gold crackers yesterday to go snap just for their party alone, is less exciting for the children to know than to discover what little silver trinkets the crackers hold for them, along with the usual bright red paper party hats.

> " 'There's the *Parrot!*' cried *Scrooge.*
> 'Green body and yellow tail, with a thing like a lettuce growing out of the top of his head; there he is!' "
>
> — CHARLES DICKENS,
> *A Christmas Carol,* 1843

YES, VIRGINIA

In 1897 an eight-year-old girl, Virginia O'Hanlon, wrote to the editor of the *New York Sun* to ask if there really is in truth a Santa Claus.

On September 21, 1897, the paper printed its answer:

Yes, Virginia, there is a Santa Claus. He exists as certainly as love and generosity and devotion exist, and you know that they abound and give to your life its highest beauty and joy. Alas! how dreary would be the world if there were no Santa Claus! It would be as dreary as if there were no Virginias. There would be no childlike faith then, no poetry, no romance to make tolerable this existence. We should have no enjoyment, except in sense and sight. The eternal light with which childhood fills the world would be extinguished.

Not believe in Santa Claus! You might as well not believe in fairies! You might get your papa to hire men to watch in all the chimneys on Christmas Eve to catch Santa Claus, but even if they did not see Santa Claus coming down, what would that prove? Nobody sees Santa Claus, but that is no sign that there is no Santa Claus. The most real things in the world are those that neither children nor men can see. Did you ever see fairies dancing on the lawn? Of course not, but that's no proof that they are not there.

You may tear apart a baby's rattle and see what makes the noise inside, but there is a veil covering the unseen world which not the strongest man, nor even the united strength of all the strongest men that ever lived, could tear apart. Only faith, fancy, poetry, love, romance, can push aside that curtain and view and picture the supernal beauty and glory beyond. Is it all real? Ah, Virginia, in all this world there is nothing else real and abiding.

No Santa Claus! Thank God! he lives, and he lives forever. A thousand years from now, Virginia, nay, ten times ten thousand years from now, he will continue to make glad the heart of childhood.

CHRISTMAS DINNER AT
THORESBY HALL

Thoresby Hall was the country seat of the celebrated American
Pierrepont family's English branch, which reached its apogee in
the early eighteenth century when Evelyn Pierrepont in rapid
succession became Earl of Kingston, Marquess of Dorchester and
Duke of Kingston-upon-Hull. The house and the 1st Duke can be
seen in a hunting painting over the sideboard. The sideboard also
boasts two framed engravings of Thoresby Hall.

Although the 1st Duke of Kingston was one of the grandest
Englishmen of his time, he was outshone by his eldest daughter,
Lady Mary Wortley Montagu, who was born at Thoresby in 1689.
She devoured the books in Thoresby's library, and at the age of
eight her learning was so esteemed that "the temple of wits," the
Kit-Cat Club, elected her a member by acclamation; she
afterward maintained that this was the happiest moment of her
life.

Lady Mary was famous as a poet, defender of women's rights,
leader of society, political commentator and shrewd investor. She
was also famous for her convoluted relationship with the poet
Alexander Pope, who persuaded her and her husband to take a
cottage near his house at Twickenham. Pope praised her in verse,
extolling her "happy air of Majesty and Youth" and

The equal Lustre of the Heavenly Mind
Where every grace with every Virtue joined
Learning not vain, and wisdom not severe
With greatness easy, and with Wit sincere.

But as one historian noted, "The close relation between a keen woman of the world and the querulous and sensitive poet was dangerous." Their friendship ended when Pope declared his passion for her and she ungenerously burst into gales of laughter. He then attacked her in a stream of poems, unjustly accusing her of usury, cruelty and even robbery.

At Lady Mary's behest, Prime Minister Sir Robert Walpole asked Pope to delete a libelous allusion from *Imitation of the First Satire of the Second Book of Horace,* but Pope refused, wrongly maintaining that Lady Mary had written a libel upon him, *A Pop upon Pope.* She responded with *Verses Addressed to an Imitator of Horace by a Lady,* which insulted Pope and his family with a brutal invective exceeded only by his own.

Lady Mary spent most of her last twenty-three years apart from her husband, living successively in Venice, Florence, Avignon, Brescia and Venice again, yet maintaining close connections with her Pierrepont family and friends through a voluminous correspondence.

This table evokes a Christmas dinner at Thoresby in the eighteenth century, when those present might have included Lady Mary and her sisters, the Countess of Mar and the Countess of Gower; her daughter, the future Marchioness of Bute; and her husband's cousin, the Marquess of Halifax.

The setting achieves a certain grandeur through the profuse display of Tiffany's exclusive "Nemours" Baccarat crystal surrounding the spectacular centerpiece, a pedestaled "Dolphin" Venetian crystal bowl by Archimede Seguso filled with fruit, Tiffany porcelain boxes, apples and beribboned pine branches. The bold rust-red borders of the Tiffany "Chrysanthemum" service plates echo the flowers on the other Tiffany "Chrysanthemum" dishes, as well as the ribbons, dried flowers and fruits decorating the sumptuous Pierrepont Christmas tree.

The "Chrysanthemum" theme is carried out by the Tiffany flat silver, as well as by the nobly proportioned "Chrysanthemum" silver letter box on the sideboard. The first such "Chrysanthemum" letter box made by Tiffany & Co. was not for a Pierrepont or even for Alexander Pope, but for Pope John XXIII.

The Christmas scene is completed by a table for two of R. Stuyvesant Pierrepont III's five young children. It is set with Tiffany "Owl and the Pussycat" baby dishes, inspired not by the querulous poet Pope but by the witty nineteenth-century English "pope" of delightfully poetic nonsense, Edward Lear.

A Victorian Christmas

Old-fashioned Christmas, commonly understood and intimately
appreciated by all, with its intoxicating visual richness, invigorating
colors and joyous attention to even the most frivolous of details, will
forever be tied in the imagination to a Victorian vision of plenty.

Christmas is an ever delightful artifice of fruitcakes and plum
puddings, of oddly shaped and decorated cookies and candies, and of
boxes and baskets of every size, shape and material tied with colored
ribbons. It invites an animating menagerie of birds and beasts to its
carnival scheme of things: doves and turkeys and parrots, horses and
reindeer, bears and cats and cows join forces on parlor carpets or under
the Christmas tree. Flowers that have no business being open in
December bloom with abandon, and everything gold or silver that can
be found is brought to the party.

For this opulent setting designed by Texas's Mrs. Oscar Wyatt, there
are ample Tiffany silver and vermeil. There is Victorian-high-style
furniture worthy of the grandest turn-of-the-century Texas cattle
barons. And on the Tiffany tea tray, there are Tiffany "Red House"
boxes, reminding all that "Home is where the heart is."

> *"... there were piles of filberts, mossy and brown, recalling, in their fragrance, ancient walks among the woods, and pleasant shufflings ankle deep through withered leaves ..."*
>
> —CHARLES DICKENS,
> *A Christmas Carol*, 1843

CHRISTMAS AT MELLERSTAIN

Perched on its balustraded terrace overlooking a postcard panorama of woods, lakes and gardens, Mellerstain, built for the 7th Earl of Haddington by Robert Adam, is one of Scotland's most noble houses.

At Christmastime the splendid display of intricate plasterwork ceilings provided by Adam attracts less attention than the traditional Mellerstain Christmas cake. A favorite of the 13th Earl's family, the cake is a delectably rich and nutty mass of ground almonds, brown sugar, eggs, butter, milk and self-rising flour, studded with chopped walnuts, filberts and sultana raisins and decorated with blanched almonds, bright red candied cherries and equally bright green angelica.

The Earl and Countess of Haddington's table is centered by a wreath of pinecones and juniper ornamented with Tiffany sterling silver horseshoes, as horses play no small role in family life at Mellerstain. A photo of the Earl and Countess sits by a Tiffany "Fleur sur Fond Gris" porcelain urn. There is a bright array of Tiffany silver, including a dog head stirrup cup.

Sitting in the library, the hunting dog on the dessert plate is trying to remember the exact wording of his favorite quotation from *Hamlet* and whether it goes "The cat will mew; the dog will have his day" or "The cat will go away, and the dog will have his Christmas cake."

T for the Toys, the Tinsel, the Tree

If every Christmas legend is to be believed, the animal population of Bethlehem the first Christmas vied with that of Noah's Ark.

There were the ox and the ass, who obligingly warmed the stable; the lambs, who provided their wool for the bedding; the cock, who crowed from midnight to dawn; the raven, who flew above the stable; the wren, who feathered the manger; and then the camels of the Three Kings: Gaspar of Tarsus; Melchior of Nubia and Arabia; and Balthazar of Ethiopia.

If that did not provide a sufficiently international list of animal motifs for Christmas decorations, Santa eventually added reindeer. Then the Victorian English, not missing a chance to promote their Indian adventures, added every creature of the subcontinent that would oblige, beginning with elephants, peacocks and tigers.

Victorian America, having a love affair with carnivals and circuses and delighting in exotic imagery, was quick to welcome all possible birds and beasts to the carnival mood of its newly discovered national holiday and feast day.

Here a toy American ox and an oriental carousel elephant are not the least bit surprised to find themselves beside a bright yellow Italian Tiffany deer. To join them, one of the children of the family has moved a Tiffany place setting to the living room carpet.

Keeping its distance, a more timid little faience cow stands under the Christmas tree on a miniature chest of drawers in case a stray Indian tiger should join the holiday festivities.

> " 'Instead of the placid ox and ass of Bethlehem,' said the vicar, slightly losing the thread of his comparisons, 'we have for companions the ravening tiger and the exotic camel, the furtive jackal and the ponderous elephant.' "
>
> —Evelyn Waugh,
> *A Handful of Dust*, 1934

YULETIDE TREASURES

With an advanced taste for marine mythology and romance, such eclectic personalities as Henri Matisse, Indira Gandhi, Erté and Helena Rubinstein have all collected grotto furniture. Constructed of boldly carved and brightly silvered and gilded giant wooden scallop shells, dolphins, conches and seahorses, this nineteenth-century near-hallucinatory manifestation of aggressive Venetian chic is a conchologist's nightmare but a collector's dream.

At this curiosities collector's Christmas dinner, decorated with a relentless taste for the stylish and the off-beat, seahorses wrap their serpentine tails about the legs of the flat shell-top dinner table, which is appropriately set with Tiffany "Wave Edge" flat silver and Venetian cabbage-leaf dishes.

The opulent five-branched Venetian glass candelabra was made for Tiffany & Co. by Pauly & Co., which about one hundred years earlier made the magnificent three-shell-backed grotto settee as well as the unique seahorse-supported, double-scallop-shell jewel casket, which the host has generously filled to overflowing with Tiffany gold, silver and pearl jewelry, to be distributed to the ladies of his family at midnight.

Giant Tiffany crystal goblets await champagne bottles. Two of the guests will receive jeweled art constructions by Reginald Case, one of a twelve-pointed Christmas star, the second of a lady equestrian acrobat who feels quite at home among the room's fabulous curiosities. At the back of the room, a pair of nineteenth-century lithographs by Sir Matthew Digby Wyatt depict curiosities in other collections.

THE SNOW QUEEN'S CHRISTMAS

Glittering, jewel-like starbursts composed of chandelier crystals by New York artist R. W.
Russell float above this theatrically romantic, wintery setting for a holiday dinner. Every
detail evokes the mythologies of the snow-covered, spirit-populated northern woods
associated with the season, and it would not be difficult to picture Santa himself with three
of his helpers sitting in the Christmas red chairs about this enchanted table fit for a fairy-
tale princess.

The cloth is completely covered with simulated leaves, and Tiffany "Autumn Leaves"
dishes are used to carry on the forest theme.

The refractive sparkle of the crystal star chandelier and its satellite is complemented by a
glittering collection of Tiffany crystal that includes "Hampton" stemware; a "Star" obelisk
and a "Ramses" obelisk (whose prismatic forms echo Russell's star structures); ribbed
Venetian candlesticks; and a "Leaf Cut" crystal vase exploding with long-stemmed snow-
white French tulips mixed with red-berried branches.

Popcorn garlands give their homey simulation of snow on the Christmas tree, which is
decorated with red satin ribbon bows and one-hundred-fifty mixed Tiffany "Swag," "Bow
Box," "Garland," "Wreath" and "Trellis" crystal ornaments.

The flat silver is Tiffany's "Faneuil," and each guest will find the gift of a Tiffany silver
turtle, frog or elephant as a place favor.

Sometime during a snowy Canadian winter in the late seventeenth century, a talented
French colonial craftsman in Quebec lavished far more skill and loving care on a simple
wooden chair than utility demanded. This chair (now in the Quebec Museum), with its
charming cutout hearts and houses and other symbols, inspired the setting's contemporary
chairs made for Tiffany's by Allan Adams of Odd Objects.

A red-nosed reindeer, whose glowing nose announces a close relationship to Rudolph, as
well as a firsthand knowledge of Santa's dinner plans, has come in through the wrought-iron
gates to inspect the table and possibly nibble on a white tulip or two—which, with a deer's
well-known predilection for garden flowers, he could confuse with part of the all-white
holiday dinner that will soon be announced.

THE SNOW QUEEN'S CHRISTMAS DINNER

> *"[The] little star was a long time flying through the air, and, at last, it fell down into the heart of a wood, where the trees were thickest, where the firs intertwined their shaggy branches and made an eerie humming noise."*
>
> —ALEXEY REMIZOV,
> *Her Star-Bear*, 1926

Surely at least two of the ladies at this glamorously appointed table celebrating winter's dress of snow and ice will be two flawless Jean Harlowesque platinum blondes wearing bias-cut white satin gowns and dripping with equally flawless Tiffany diamonds.

The men will be dapper and debonair and may appear wearing white ties just for the simple fun of it.

The assembly may discuss the famed Pecci-Blunt Surrealist Ball given in Paris in 1922, at which Man Ray projected black-and-white movies on the all-white-clothed guests as they danced after dinner.

Not to disappoint the moment's winter magic, the dinner itself will be entirely white.

To begin, there will be champagne and a chilled salad of crab and lobster meat, finely chopped celery and water chestnuts, all mixed with a little mayonnaise and sour cream and flavored with crushed Szechwan peppercorns and a hint of grated gingerroot.

The main course will be poached chicken breasts in a rich cream sauce filled with sliced sautéed white mushrooms and pearl onions. The chicken will be served with braised salsify and a potato-and-artichoke-heart purée, and accompanied by a Puligny-Montrachet.

There will be a Belgian endive salad with fresh chèvre; and to finish, the dessert will be poached pears served with vanilla bean ice cream and a hot white chocolate sauce flavored with a bit of cognac.

A similar dinner cooked by surrealist muse Lee Miller Penrose and John Loring was served in New York at an all-white party in 1972 commemorating the Man Ray retrospective at the New York Cultural Center, as well as commemorating the fiftieth anniversary of the Pecci-Blunt ball.

A Southern
Christmas

Christmas in the southern American states takes on a more boisterous and luxuriant sensuality than in its New England counterparts. It has a polish and elegance recalling the indulgent lifestyle of Regency England or Restoration France rather than the homey, cozy, folkloric charm of northern Victorian-style Christmases.

There are less likely to be party-favor-filled paper Christmas crackers on the dinner table than there are to be firecrackers outdoors, as the true Southerner's love of fireworks for every festivity extends to Christmas.

The decorations, too, take on different hues, red giving way to yellow and pink. And instead of nuts and dried fruits, lusciously fresh hothouse grapes are a necessary ornament to every dining room.

Ornate neo-Renaissance silverware such as Tiffany "Olympian" is at home on Southern tables, and the bright-colored Imari wares of New England give way to more formal gold-and-white china patterns. Here Regency-style "Palm" silver candlesticks from Tiffany's further contribute to the warm look of the South.

Traditional foods themselves have their own regional character and the Southern Christmas should not be without spoon bread, baked creamed celery with almonds, "Sally Lunn" bread, oyster pie, johnnycakes, and "Tipsy Pudding," or a custard-filled "Washington Pie," or spiced-orange-and-cognac "Café Brûlot" to finish off the meal.

". . . there were bunches of grapes, made, in the shopkeepers' benevolence, to dangle from conspicuous hooks that people's mouths might water gratis as they passed . . ."

—CHARLES DICKENS,
A Christmas Carol, 1843

CHRISTMAS IN THE NURSERY

*"And he's sure to have with him
a bundle of toys
For the nice little girls and
the good little boys.
And he would be kind to them
all if he could,
But he gives his nice presents
to none but the good."*

GEORGE P. WEBSTER,
Santa Claus and His Works, 1870

This adamantly aristocratic nursery with its Victorian neo-Gothic mood evokes the royal nursery at Windsor Castle on December 25, 1841, when Queen Victoria and Prince Albert celebrated the first Christmas of their new son, Prince Albert Edward (later Edward VII).

Albert Edward was the first male heir apparent born in England since 1762, and in the male-chauvinist society curiously ruled over by a matriarch, his mother, his birth was seen by the English as a semi-miraculous augury of good fortune. To celebrate, his German father, Prince Albert of Saxe-Coburg-Gotha, had that German phenomenon, a Christmas tree, set up at Windsor to delight his firstborn son, and with the Christmas tree inevitably followed the Teutonic image of Santa Claus.

Through the enthusiastic press coverage it received at the time, the tree was to delight not only the infant crown prince but the rest of England as well; and as a result, the Christmas tree in England and America will forever be an essentially Victorian concept.

By no coincidence, when Charles Dickens returned to England six months later in mid-1842 after a tour of America, he soon focused his literary attentions on England's own newfound focus on Christmas. As a result of this, in the fall of 1843 he sat down to write *A Christmas Carol*, which was put on sale in London on December 19 of that year. The first edition of six thousand copies sold out that day.

Dickens's subtitle, *Being a Ghost Story of Christmas,* was a departure from the evocations of nostalgic, and most probably imaginary, English Christmases that he had attempted in *The Pickwick Papers* (1836–37), in which he characterized Christmas in early-nineteenth-century England as a season of "hospitality, merriment, and open-heartedness" joined by "companionship and mutual good-will."

Dickens's *Ghost Story* suggests a less traditional Gothic tale, including three rather eerie variants of Santa in keeping with the neo-Gothic spirit of the day, which was a radical departure from *The Pickwick Papers* and 1837, the final year of the undistinguished eat, drink and be merry reign of Victoria's uncle William IV.

The neo-Gothic crib (see pages 92–93), which once belonged to America's near-royal Astor family, the French neo-Gothic birdcage and the painted medallion of Gothic ruins on the Napoleon III papier-mâché chairback all recall that first modern English Christmas at the Gothic castle of Windsor in 1841, when the Gothic Revival led by Sir Charles Barry and A. W. N. Pugin had just begun.

The new movement was at the dawn of an all-encompassing cultural revolution that spawned the Arts and Crafts Movement, along with a new aesthetic and intellectual vibrancy that was to spread over Western Europe and America.

One of its manifestations was the exploration of new materials, such as papier-mâché, or the etched and painted plate-glass panels of this setting's folding screen, which could provide an aesthetically pleasing and inexpensive way to make art available to the public, a concept that did not pass unnoticed by Tiffany's founder Charles Lewis Tiffany or his Arts and Crafts–championing son, Louis Comfort Tiffany.

The Tiffany "Biedermeier" ceramics used here on the nursery table recall another early phase of this nineteenth-century vision of bringing good design to "everyman" which first manifested itself in Eastern Europe in the Biedermeier style.

A MEDIEVAL
CHRISTMAS

*". . . the sticks of cinnamon so long and
straight, the other spices so delicious,
the candied fruits so caked and spotted
with molten sugar as to make the
coldest lookers-on feel faint . . ."*

— CHARLES DICKENS,
A Christmas Carol, 1843

Maxime de la Falaise's *Seven Centuries of English Cooking* is one of
the twentieth century's most intriguing cookbooks, as it chronicles
the culinary achievements of "cooks, and scribes and prelates of
bygone days" and brings them all alive again.

Here Maxime de la Falaise's Christmas table offers a witty
allusion to those pre-Tiffany table-setting days when bread
trenchers rather than china plates were popular for feasting.

In keeping with her great talent at accessorizing, her Tiffany
"Faneuil" flat silver stuck into a small beehive has been made into an
original table ornament to recall the days when revelers drank mead
made from wheat and honey, as well as to allude to the medieval
legend that bees hum carols at midnight on Christmas Eve.

Crystallized ginger in a Tiffany ceramic gourd jar may serve as a
reminder that there are not one but two recipes for gingerbread in
her cookbook. The fifteenth-century recipe notes the decorative
suggestion that "in the Middle Ages gingerbread would sometimes
be covered with gold leaf."

The lady apples may serve to remind that, as Maxime de la
Falaise gratefully acknowledges, her fellow cookbook author and
editor of *Seven Centuries of English Cooking,* Arabella Boxer,
"courageously excised twenty-five apple pies from one century
alone!"

NEW YORK—DECEMBER 25

The interior ornament of a typical nineteenth-century New York town house's family rooms quite invariably centered on a simply designed but amply proportioned white marble fireplace. Its wide stone mantle offered no home for hanging Christmas stockings but gave ample opportunity to pile on a glorious display of pine boughs, decorated with lady apples, pomegranates, gold-painted walnuts and red ribbons. To this could be added Tiffany silver bowls of paper-white narcissus, small pale blue gift boxes tied with more red ribbons and a pair of red Christmas candles held in candlesticks meant to be used only at the holiday season, like the Tiffany "Christmas Tree" Venetian crystal candleholders used here.

There would, in the best of cases, be an elaborately carved gilt-wood console table to hold punch bowls and pitchers of holiday drinks; and if good luck continued, a cut-crystal galleon might glide through the air above the center table to animate and illuminate the room and delight the children.

The table could have a bright red damask cloth and a machine-made neomedieval tapestry overlay for the Christmas dinner. Tiffany "Corinthian Column" silver candlesticks with more red candles would do very well, as would as many Tiffany "Holly" ceramics as would fit on the table and console together.

In such a setting of relatively sober domestic splendor, there would be no reason not to have two Christmas trees instead of one. The two trees would then provide obvious opportunities for even more stacks of blue boxes tied with even more red ribbons than the children of the house thought imaginable.

SANTA-CLAUSVILLE

In the dreams of children, Christmas always tends to take place in the endless pine-and-birch forests of the north, such as those that cover Scandinavia.

There bears play among the stars on a winter's night. There is always snow about, but also a warm fire in a bright red wood-burning stove, and a Christmas tree, and presents and a special table for the children with no food other than cakes and puddings and gingerbread and candy.

Parents must keep to their own table to eat all the caviar and gravlax and other fishy things that grown-ups like, served out of a Tiffany "Salmon" tureen onto Tiffany "Trout" plates. And while the children drink great pots of hot chocolate keeping warm on the stove, their parents can have all the iced vodka and champagne they can drink out of Tiffany "57th Street" Swedish glasses.

> " 'But all that the children could hear was a ringing of bells.'
> " 'You mean that the postman went rat-a-tat-tat and the doors rang?'
> " 'I mean that the bells that the children could hear were inside them.' "
>
> —DYLAN THOMAS,
> *A Child's Christmas in Wales,* 1950

THE THREE BEARS' CHRISTMAS

> *"They would have asked her to breakfast; for they were good Bears—a little rough or so, as the manner of Bears is, but for all that very good natured and hospitable."*
>
> —ROBERT SOUTHEY,
> *Story of the Three Bears,* 1834

International society's chief minstrel, Peter Duchin, and his beautiful muse, Brooke Hayward, know better than anyone the secrets of setting the stage for a memorable evening.

Their script tonight calls for a winter soirée with the world-famous Three Bears. The elks, the rams and a few sociable Hampshire pigs dressed to the nines in their formal black and white, as is the manner of well-bred Hampshires, are all invited.

A lizard and a turtle from goodness knows where join the party, and to make them feel at home, the table setting includes a pair of Tiffany vermeil crab candlesticks.

There are blue gels on the spots for moonlight and plenty of artificial snow.

Tiffany "Black Shoulder" covered porridge tureens are provided for the Great, Huge Bear and the Middle-Sized Bear. A pot of honey in lieu of a star tops the bears' Christmas "sweetmeat tree," and plenty of beer will be drunk from Tiffany champagne flutes.

After dinner the Great, Huge Bear will play with great, huge cards and the Middle-Sized Bear will dance to the music of Peter Duchin's orchestra.

A TIFFANY FAMILY CHRISTMAS

Tiffany's founder, Charles Lewis Tiffany, as painted by the great American Impressionist William Merritt Chase shortly before Christmas 1901, presides over this lavishly appointed setting for Christmas dinner.

Red—the color of love and fire, the color of celebration, December's color—has since ancient Druid and Roman times been combined at year-end winter festivals with nature's green, symbolic of regeneration and the promise of another spring. They are offset here by the radiant gold of the sun

and stars and of candlelight and by the symbolically pure white of snow to make up the Christmas palette of this table honoring the Tiffany family's love of festivity, of aesthetic excitement and of excellence in all things.

While the red plaid bows and fabrics evoke a Victorian Christmas at the English Royal Family's Scottish castle of Balmoral, the popcorn garland on the tree and the cranberries on the table, along with the Tiffany "English King" flat silver and "Tiffany

Garland" holiday china, identify this as the setting of
a most American "royal" family.

Louis Comfort Tiffany, who designed the
setting's sterling silver three-handled floriform vase,
indulged a sense of opulence that inspired his
relations to call him "Kubla Khan." It would not be
difficult to picture him presiding pasha-like over
dinner from the setting's canopied red-, green- and
gold-striped Regency chair.

> "*. . . he didn't believe there ever was such a
> goose cooked. Its tenderness and flavour,
> size and cheapness, were the themes of
> universal admiration.*"
>
> —CHARLES DICKENS,
> *A Christmas Carol,* 1843

LE CROQUEMBOUCHE

> *"Christmas is green and general like all great works of the imagination, swelling from minute private sentiments in the desert, a wreath around our intimacy like children's voices in a park."*
>
> —FRANK O'HARA,
> *Christmas Card to Grace Hartigan,* 1954

In the mid-1750s, Louis XV's Royal Porcelain Manufactory at Vincennes on the eastern outskirts of Paris created a new rich, pale green porcelain enamel color for Madame de Pompadour, Louis's beautiful young "Protectress of the Arts" and the inspired directress and propagandist of Vincennes.

Here Mrs. Ezra Zilkha, frequent chairman of the Metropolitan Opera's Opening Night Gala Committee and one of America's leading protectresses and propagandists of the arts, uses *le vert Louis Quinze* to set the discreetly luxurious tone of a holiday season supper after the opera. The subtlety and variety of greens bring depth and nuance to the evening's décor.

Mrs. Zilkha's round table is skirted with gold mesh and set with Tiffany Louis XV–style "Provence" flatware; gadrooned sterling silver service plates; and green "Cardinale" handpainted china, decorated in Tiffany's own studios in Paris. The table's centerpiece, a tall Venetian-glass-footed cup, is filled with red and green lady apples and holds a profusion of red berries, green orchids, holly and ivy.

The ivy adds its pleasant variegated green and is symbolic of regeneration in the mythology of midwinter festivities. The holly, symbolic of foresight, has been involved since ancient Roman times in winter-solstice festivities too numerous and too folkloric to mention.

Together, the holly and the ivy inspired a traditional English carol in which the ivy has only a walk-on part, while the holly shows off not only its white blossoms and red berries but its sharp "prickles" and bitter bark as well; all to what avail is not made entirely clear by the end of *The Holly and the Ivy* carol. This, of course, is not surprising, as English carolers have been known on Christmas Eve to stick sprigs of holly on top of beehives and sing such carols to the doubtlessly bewildered inhabitants, who nonetheless obligingly hum along in response.

The French, being more Cartesian and therefore more practical and logical, make honey-colored, beehive-shaped cakes to celebrate Christmas Eve.

Atop Mrs. Zilkha's Louis XV commode sideboard, a Venetian glass dolphin compote of regal proportions shows off a towering *croquembouche,* the traditional beehive-shaped holiday party dessert of France.

The architecture of the *croquembouche,* that mechanical marvel of French cuisine, is achieved by attaching cream puffs filled with a mixture of whipped cream and *crème pâtissière* with a "mortar" of hot caramelized sugar. Purists prefer the filling to be flavored with only a bit of vanilla; however, alternate fillings use chocolate and even crushed almonds, walnuts, pecans or hazelnuts or, in honor of the season, crushed peppermint candy canes.

A green-and-gold eighteenth-century polychromed leather chinoiserie panel and the green stamped-velvet upholstery on the Louis XV armchairs lend additional background greens.

BOXING DAY

The country look of England is built of waxed pine and polished oak and walnut, of Yorkshire ladder-back chairs and pine Welsh dressers displaying cobalt-blue-and-white Staffordshire transfer wares. The dresser that both stores and exhibits the treasures of the English kitchen or dining room, when there is one, is incomplete without its collection of mismatched milk and cream pitchers, its mugs hanging from cup hooks below its shelves, and its menagerie of painted ceramic farm animals—cows, and perhaps a bull; poultry; and even a dog or two.

Here in a Boxing Day setting by America's favorite English singing star of stage and screen, Angela Lansbury, all the familiar English country furnishings and ornaments are in their proper places.

The tea party worthy of her *Beauty and the Beast* character, Mrs. Potts, includes both a Tiffany silver hot water kettle and a "Drab Ware" neoclassic teapot. There are animated cartoon-colored paper crackers for each of her guests, and naturally there is the requisite English marzipan-and-fondant-coated Christmas fruitcake decorated with very English sprigs of holly and topped by a tiny Christmas tree and a mother and baby reindeer.

A symbolic lion inspects the table from the dresser to make sure there are ample scones and biscuits and plenty of pots of jam.

> *"Everyone ate a great deal and became slightly torpid towards Boxing Day evening; silver ladles of burning brandy went around the table, crackers were pulled and opened . . ."*
>
> —EVELYN WAUGH,
> *A Handful of Dust*, 1934

A VERY FORMAL CELEBRATION

A splendid three-tiered floral topiary tree composed of all-red roses, carnations, African daisies, asters, poppies and chrysanthemums is punctuated by pale blue anemones and scabiosa, then studded with pearls and finally tied with tiny gold ribbon bows to set the very French and very formal party mood of this Christmas table.

The ikated French silk taffeta plaid table cover unites a sumptuous array of Tiffany china, crystal and silver that boasts "English King" flat silver and "Nemours" Baccarat crystal water goblets, wineglasses and champagne flutes. There are Tiffany "Escalier de Cristal" porcelain plates and cups, whose blue-and-gold arcades over jewel-like flowers recall the arcades of Paris's Palais Royal, where the Paris porcelain shop, also named Escalier de Cristal, that first produced this pattern in the 1830s was located.

There are four matching Tiffany French Regency–style sterling silver candlesticks, all hand-chased with masks and scallop shells that echo the scallop shell on the room's French Regency–style marble mantelpiece.

The hand-lettered menu announces the main course of dinner as a most French "Rabbit with Wild Mushrooms," followed by an equally French "Black Currant Sorbet."

> "... as a pretty child, before me, delightedly whispered to another pretty child, her bosom friend, 'There was everything, and more.' "
>
> —CHARLES DICKENS,
> A Christmas Tree, 1850

Christmas Dinner
1987

...omme of Beef
...m with Cumberland Sauce

... with Wild Mushrooms
...ucumber with Dill
...Potatoes Dauphinoise

...Black Currant Sorbet
Christmas Cake

Mr John Ausenschaft

RED-AND-WHITE
BREAKFAST

> *"Yet was there an air of cheerfulness abroad that the clearest summer air and brightest summer sun might have endeavoured to diffuse in vain."*
>
> —CHARLES DICKENS,
> *A Christmas Carol*, 1843

Has a little blond Swedish girl wearing a white dress with a red sash and balancing a crown of evergreens and red candles on her head just delivered coffee and cakes, as little blond Swedish girls do on St. Lucia's Day to begin the Christmas season? Or is the sunny mood more Austrian? After all, the white-lacquered rectilinear Art Nouveau chairs are in the 1910 style of Vienna, and aren't red and white the colors of Austria? And then, too, there are brioches, recalling the Austrian Queen of France's notorious and unfortunate quip, *"Qu'ils mangent de la brioche!"* The morning, however, is far too cheery for that sort of association. But then there is Tiffany "Hampton" silver; there is cranberry juice to drink; and there is Tiffany "Red Vine" bone china, whose leaves coordinate so perfectly with the crisp red-and-white "granny print" chintz tablecloth, to say that this is, after all, a most American Christmas breakfast.

A SPLENDID DINNER

Chinoiserie and Christmas trees have much in common, for both favor the fanciful and outlandish over the logical and ordered, and both are easily accessible to the innocent outlook of children while still satisfying the necessity of fantasy for the not-so-innocent outlook of adults; and both have a careless and disorderly grace that is both impressive and surprising.

Although chinoiserie is a European phenomenon, the Chinese might once have had a phrase for such flights of decorative fancy that could have been pronounced something like "Sa-lo-kwai-chi." This the seventeenth-century English turned into a veritable Christmas tree of a word, "Sharawadgi," which embraced all things of oriental design origin that were tastefully enlivened by disorder.

Sir William Temple described the Chinese style that would be translated into the delightful, if improbable, juxtapositions of imagery both oriental and European that became known as chinoiserie in his *Gardens of Epicurus* of 1685:

Their [the Chinese] greatest reach of Imagination is employed in contriving Figures, where the Beauty shall be great and strike the Eye, but without any order or disposition of parts, that shall be commonly or easily observ'd. And though we have hardly any Notion of this sort of Beauty, yet they have a particular Word to express it; and where they find it hit their Eye at first sight, they say the Sharawadgi is fine or is admirable, or any such expression of Esteem . . . but I should hardly advise any of these Attempts . . . among us; they are Adventures of too hard achievement for any common Hands; and tho there may be more Honour if they succeed well, yet there is more Dishonour if they fail, and 'tis twenty to one they will.

Here in this setting a glorious Christmas tree "without any order or disposition of parts," as Christmas trees usually are, is decorated with a profusion of roses, dried hydrangeas, Tiffany silver teddy bear ornaments, gold-paper leaves, red silk bows and spiral-striped Venetian glass balls. Looking as if contrived by Santa Claus in his old role of Lord of Misrule and Disorder, it makes a splendid backdrop for this holiday dinner table centered on a Tiffany "Pagoda" silver chinoiserie centerpiece inhabited by three very Western bouquets of white tulips in cut-crystal vases.

There is "Hampton" gold vermeil flatware, and the china is Tiffany "Palmier d'Or" porcelain, whose chinoiserie motifs include palm trees, more pagodas and little gold Chinamen going about "Adventures of too hard achievement" to mention at this festive dinner where the Sharawadgi is admirable.

A Holiday Luncheon
in the City

> " 'It snowed last year, too. I made a snowman
> and my brother knocked it down and
> I knocked my brother down
> and then we had tea.' "
>
> —Dylan Thomas,
> *A Child's Christmas in Wales,* 1950

Since it was introduced in the mid-1950s, Tiffany's "Cirque Chinois" porcelain pattern has delighted everyone. Based on old Paris porcelain prototypes from around 1800, its witty mixture of chinoiserie and end-of-the-eighteenth-century neoclassicism allows it to flourish in the most diverse décors.

Here its gaily dressed Chinese children carry on under blue palm trees and gold acacias in an animated formal procession. They ride in dragon chariots pulled by fabulous winged monsters, juggle, argue, balance on teeter-totters and play on pipes.

In this setting's updated and adamantly urban neoclassic décor, the once lacquered and gilded English Regency open-arm chairs and console sideboard have been stripped down to the wood—rope-pattern crest rails, reeded legs and all—in a design statement as urbane and stylishly delinquent as the antics of the children on the "Cirque Chinois" porcelains. An army of red and white amaryllises and paper-white narcissus in another procession promotes a stylistic mixture of Christmas and neoclassicism, which is seconded by the generously scaled Christmas wreath.

THE PARTNERS' HOLIDAY BRUNCH

Amid the stately appointments of this elegant architecture and design office, a Tiffany sterling silver rat has taken up its position just next to the Christmas cake on the partners' lunch table, and is lecturing a pair of Tiffany silver mice on the fine points of refurbishing an Upper East Side New York Renaissance Revival mansion. All three will then grab pieces of the prettily frosted cake.

Rats and mice, unfestive as they might seem, occupied a prominent place in Victorian Christmas illustration. Always in a celebratory mood, despite their meager circumstances, they affirmed once again that the spirit of Christmas is independent of finance and social order. That may or may not be the comment they are making here, while pursuing their own ends among the handsome Tiffany table furnishings.

Coffee waits on a "pineapple" silver tray that echoes the table's centerpiece bowl of baby pink and green-leaved pineapples.

The partners have exchanged Tiffany gifts appropriate for business, including a perpetual calendar, a silver stamp box and letter opener, a travel clock and "Tiffany" fragrance, whose architectural bottle recalling Tiffany's American Art Deco store at Fifty-seventh Street and Fifth Avenue pleases all the design partners.

> *"I can never remember whether it snowed for six days and six nights when I was twelve or whether it snowed for twelve days and twelve nights when I was six."*
>
> — DYLAN THOMAS,
> *A Child's Christmas in Wales*, 1950

'TIS THE SEASON
TO BE FESTIVE

> *"Johnny wants a pair of skates;*
>
> *Susy wants a dolly;*
>
> *Nellie wants a storybook;*
>
> *She thinks dolls are folly."*
>
> —ANONYMOUS,
> *Jolly Old St. Nicholas*

The Mediterranean port city of Marseilles enjoyed an animated and intensely cosmopolitan life during the latter part of the eighteenth century, and its ceramics with their fresh and delicate floral patterns were exported to all of Europe. Designed by local painters trained at Louis XV's and Louis XVI's Royal Academy of Painting in Marseilles, they had a refinement and grace that found favor even at the difficult and discriminating court of Versailles.

The more proletarian tastes of the nineteenth century had little use for aristocratic charm, and Marseilles's products fell into disuse until the 1906 Colonial Exposition held in Marseilles. There the world was reintroduced to the supple green sprigs and undulating stems of field flowers painted with a refreshingly light touch in clear Mediterranean colors. And since 1906, Marseilles's so beautiful patterns with their refined country charm have again become a classic of table design vocabulary.

Here the table is set with Tiffany Louis XVI–style "Green Sprig" dishes, with covered soup bowls for the holiday meal's traditional Marseilles bouillabaisse. There are, appropriately, "Provence" flat silver and a long-standing favorite Tiffany Christmas gift, a "Cow Tureen" painted with the blue-and-green Marseilles *décor de rose violette* typical of the eighteenth-century manufacturing of Joseph Fauchier.

WRITING THANK-YOU NOTES

When the first Tiffany store opened for business at 259 Broadway on September 21, 1837, stationery and "fancy goods" were its only offerings to the New York public; and although Tiffany's merchandise selections are now far more focused on jewelry and table furnishings, Tiffany's Stationery Department remains a premier source of fine American personal and business writing and note paper, invitations and, of course, engraved Christmas and Hanukkah cards.

One of the civilized pleasures of the holiday season is the exercise of the sociable art of the thank-you note, written in appreciation for gifts, for holiday entertainments, for help with the season's charitable events, or simply in response to a friend's Christmas letter.

Here, seated on a Louis XVI gilded armchair at a Louis XV writing desk *à dos d'âne,* the lady of the house has prepared for this pleasurable annual task.

Tiffany "T-Clip" silver pens and a silver letter opener are held in a "Princess Astrid" porcelain box. There is a Tiffany magnifying glass to decipher difficult handwriting, as well as a silver box of stamps. Tea and a scone are served with "Halcyon" china, and the desk's pigeonholes offer a selection of Tiffany hand-bordered note cards which come in pale blue, ecru or white and which might be engraved with monograms or addresses, coats of arms or personalized drawings in any of dozens of colors.

In case a moment of writer's block sets in and inspiration for another *bon mot* fails, there is a crystal decanter filled with excellent cognac.

> "*They were not forty children conducting themselves like one, but every child was conducting itself like forty. The consequences were uproarious beyond belief.*"
>
> —CHARLES DICKENS,
> *A Christmas Carol*, 1843

CHILDREN'S PARTY
AT FLOORS CASTLE

From the colorful plastic water pistols at their places, it would not be obvious that this children's Christmas table is set for no lesser youths than Charles Robert George, Marquess of Bowmont and Cessford, and his two siblings, Lord Edward Arthur Gerald Innes Ker and Lady Rosanagh Viola Alexandra Innes Ker, the children of the 10th Duke of Roxburghe.

Their mother, née Lady Jane Grosvenor, encourages all manner of fun and revelry at the Christmas table, and knows that a shot from a water pistol makes an excellent punctuation mark in the party conversation of even the most noble children.

Less Christmas-spirited relations might uncharitably remind each other that, after all, the young Lords (and Lady) of Misrule had an American great-grandmother, May Goelet, heir of New York's nineteenth-century schooner-racing millionaire Ogden Goelet. He would, however, undoubtedly have approved of his great-great-grandchildren's uproarious behavior.

The children's Christmas table is set with Tiffany "Audubon" flat silver and "Princess Astrid" porcelain. Crepe paper Christmas balls conceal coins and small party favors, and each child has a Tiffany "King Cole" silver cup for refilling water pistols.

The Goelet Cup for Schooners, with its spirited Neptune brandishing a trident in lieu of a Roxburghe water pistol, was made by Tiffany's for Ogden Goelet in 1884 and is now in the New York Yacht Club.

THE DAY AFTER CHRISTMAS

*"The walls and ceiling were so hung
with living green, that it looked
a perfect grove . . ."*

— CHARLES DICKENS,
A Christmas Carol, 1843

Santa's sleigh-load of toys has been distributed, stockings have been emptied and Christmas crackers pulled, the turkey has been stuffed and roasted and partially devoured, the pudding has been set ablaze, and a bit of it may even have been eaten.

The rest of the pudding will keep for a while if wrapped in a brandy-soaked cloth and kept cold; but the day after Christmas, there is often much discussion as to what to do with the leftover turkey meat, which could remain in considerable quantity.

There are the time-honored American solutions of creamed turkey and potato hash; turkey curry; or turkey croquettes with chopped-hard-boiled-egg sauce.

In Tuscany the Italians have their own solution for leftover meats. They re-serve them in a light tomato sauce laced with sautéed onions. Turkey, however, adapts better to a Tuscan *lesso rifatto con olive* (leftovers recooked with olives), which is made by sautéeing a few cloves of finely chopped garlic with some salt in a generous amount of olive oil, adding peeled and seeded ripe tomatoes and lots of oil-cured Tuscan black olives, and allowing this sauce to simmer until the mixture is reduced by a third. Then the turkey, cut into small chunks, is added; and when it is all hot, it is served up with pasta.

The Venetians have their own traditional and quite unique recipe for roast turkey that serves as well for leftovers as for a fresh roast bird. The Venetian *tacchinella al melograno* (turkey with pomegranate) can be made by simply reheating roast turkey and serving it with a sauce made by finely chopping one medium onion per pound of turkey meat, adding fresh (or dried) rosemary, and sautéeing it in olive oil. Leftover giblet gravy is then added to the onion and rosemary, and the sauce is thinned with fresh pomegranate juice made by pressing the pulpy seeds from pomegranates, which so frequently appear in today's Christmas decorations. (In old Venetian dialect, this intriguing fruit enjoyed the name *malgaragno* and was used to flavor many game birds. Its bright pink seeds also make a festive decoration sprinkled around the edges of a platter.)

The French find another solution to the leftover problem with a *salade d'olivier,* made with cold turkey rather than with the more usual roast veal. This fine dish can be made with cold boiled small potatoes cut into chunks; roughly chopped celery; chopped mild dill pickles; peeled, seeded and finely chopped French cucumber; diced turkey; and well-seasoned homemade mayonnaise made with French olive oil.

Grander French households might suggest taking thin slices of cold breast meat of turkey; partially spreading them with "leftover" foie gras mashed with a bit of cream; forming them into neat packets; and glazing them with a white chaud-froid sauce. They can then be decorated with small slices of black truffle, if they are for a formal occasion.

Here the post-Christmas table is set for whichever of these dishes may please the cook of the house. An Art Deco Raoul Dufy print cloth's leafy patterns refresh the Christmas greens and flowers. Dishes and crystal candleholders from Tiffany's Frank Lloyd Wright Collection bring their enlivening twentieth-century geometries; and there is American Art Deco Tiffany "Century" flat silver.

A RED, WHITE AND BLUE DINNER

Sitting over a regal George II marble-mosaic-topped pine console, the great red macaw in this setting's 1860s still life painting is as proud of his own dazzling plumage and his two baskets laden with melons, grapes, peaches and a pineapple as the formal dinner table is of its Christmas red damask cloth and its explosive bouquet of white Hawaiian orchids. The classic table furnishings of Tiffany "English King" flat silver; blue, red and gold Imari china; and hand-cut Irish crystal wineglasses lend a dignity to the setting, designed by New York and Palm Beach's glamorous socialite Mrs. T. Suffern Tailer in an American high style worthy of a presidential state dinner.

The first American President, George Washington, had neither so grand a Christmas table nor even a capital city. Not a great deal is known of his first presidential Christmas "levee" except that it took place in Philadelphia and that the President wore black velvet knee breeches and accessorized his costume with silver shoe buckles and a sword in a white leather scabbard.

There was, no doubt, one of Martha Washington's "Great Cakes," which was a mammoth fruitcake made with forty eggs; four pounds of butter; four pounds of sugar; five pounds of flour; five pounds of mixed white raisins, currants, orange and lemon peel, citron and angelica; one-half ounce of mace; a whole nutmeg, grated; a half-pint of wine and a half-pint of brandy. And there must have been "George Washington Eggnog," made with brandy, rye whiskey, sherry and Jamaica rum, all four together with the usual eggs, cream and sugar.

Thomas Jefferson's more cultivated international Christmas menus might have been better suited to Mrs. Tailer's highly cultivated décor. His French chef introduced Washington, D.C., to Dutch waffles, French ice cream, Italian macaroni, imported cheeses and fine French wines.

Later, Andrew Jackson was to further refine White House Christmases with his own French chef's confections of ices in the form of fruits and corn and squash; and in honor of Christmas, there were even toy animals and a reindeer made entirely from ices. An enthusiastic Dolly Madison is said to have inaccurately, but with all good intentions, described one of these Jackson family midwinter celebrations as reminiscent of *A Midsummer Night's Dream.*

And so presidential Christmases progressed. In the 1850s, Franklin Pierce surprised Washington with an ornamented "German Tree." Benjamin Harrison around 1890 announced that people had a "duty . . . to make merry," and announced that he, too, would have an "old-fashioned Christmas Tree," despite the fact that the fashion of Christmas trees was only some forty years old in America.

In the 1920s, the Calvin Coolidges had not one, but two large trees, one in the Blue Room and the second upstairs; and in 1923, President Coolidge pressed a switch to light the first "National Christmas Tree" on the White House lawn. Some years later, Franklin D. Roosevelt, caught up in the extroversion of the season's feelings, decided to read Charles Dickens's *A Christmas Carol* aloud to his children and grandchildren after Christmas dinner.

Even the red macaw would have turned from his melons and pineapple and taken notice of that.

GRACIE MANSION, 1984

With this 1984 holiday dinner setting for New York's Mayor Edward Koch, Tiffany & Co. celebrated the just-completed refurbishment of Gracie Mansion, residence of the mayors of New York City. The dining room's scenic wallpaper, showing architectural monuments among parks and riverbanks, was printed in 1830 by Charles Dufour in Paris and re-created by muralist Erik Filban for this holiday setting.

The American Empire pier table from Gracie Mansion's dining room dates from 1840. The easel beside it was made about 1880 by Herter Brothers, a prominent New York furniture maker and decorating firm of the time. On the easel there is a reproduction of an aquatint in Gracie Mansion's parlor, *Hell Gate.* Printed in 1815 by English-born artist John Hill as part of his portfolio *Twenty Scenic Views of North America,* it shows the East River looking north as seen from Gracie Mansion's garden more than one hundred eighty years ago.

The plates on the dining table bear the seal of the City of New York in blue and gold and were designed by Tiffany & Co. exclusively for Gracie Mansion. The Tiffany "Audubon" flat silver, like the plates, was presented to the mansion by Tiffany's in 1984.

The Tiffany silver monteith bowl at the center of the table is surrounded with bittersweet, and the chandelier above is covered with evergreens to celebrate the holiday season.

The Children Have
a Formal Tea Party

The children's table is set with Tiffany "Green Sprig" and "Biedermeier" potteries and "Flemish" flat silver, but pineapples in the centerpiece and the intense little verbenas on the printed cotton cloth hint at a subtropical Christmas Eve.

Perhaps it is Mexico and in a moment strings of bright little *niñitos* lights will appear, lighting the garden bushes around the table.

The children will drink mugs of hot chocolate and eat a custard-filled cake, and someone will tell the story of the humble little Mexican child and the *flor de fuego* or *flor de la Nochebuena*—the story of how the child was too poor to have a Christmas Eve gift to take to the shrine of the Virgin of Guadalupe, of how she gathered up some stems of a plant that was growing by the roadside as the Christmas procession was entering the church, and of how she offered her humble handful of weeds to the Virgin.

All the children know the end of the story. Once in the church, the leaves of the poor child's offering turned out to be as red as flames and at their center were little yellow flowers like stars.

Joel Roberts Poinsett, the U.S. Minister to Mexico from 1825 to 1829, heard the same story and took cuttings of the miraculous plant back to his native South Carolina in 1829.

Since then, the flower that bears his name, the poinsettia, has become as inseparable from American Christmas as Santa Claus.

BREAKFAST IN BED
AT CLIVEDEN PLACE

"She went to bed early, so as to let Santa Claus have a chance at the stockings . . ."

—WILLIAM DEAN HOWELLS,
Christmas Every Day, 1892

The Right Honourable William Waldorf Astor, 4th Viscount Astor, presided over this re-creation of a Christmas morning breakfast in bed at Cliveden Place, recalling the days of his grandmother, the legendary Nancy Astor.

A torsade of Tiffany pearls with a gold-and-diamond barrel clasp, presumably a Christmas gift from Nancy Astor's husband, Waldorf Astor, has arrived with the silver breakfast tray, while a Tiffany sterling silver hand mirror, comb and brush set wait on the skirted table at the foot of the bed along with a black-and-gold "Nuits de Chine" porcelain chinoiserie box filled with potpourri and a Tiffany engine-turned picture frame holding a photo of the Astors' home, Cliveden Place.

The monogrammed pillow slips, which belonged to Lady Astor, are from the collections of the Cliveden Place Historic Trust.

Nancy Langhorne was born in Albemarle County, Virginia, in 1879. Her blazing blue eyes and high spirits riveted attention. A fearless rider, she occasionally fell while jumping her mare Queen Bee over the high fences in the family orchard, but went on to win many competitions in county horse shows, once shouting to a rival, "Wake up your horse and tell him the show is on."

In 1906 she married Waldorf Astor, only heir of William Waldorf Astor, a stupendously rich New Yorker who had emigrated to England in 1890. As a wedding present, her father-in-law gave the newlyweds Cliveden Place, a beautiful seventeenth-century estate that had once belonged to the Dukes of Buckingham and Dukes of Westminster. Its gigantic Italian Renaissance–style house,

overlooking the Thames, was designed in 1850 by Sir Charles Barry. Shortly after they moved in, King Edward VII paid the new Lady Astor a visit and "the show was on" in earnest.

Nancy Astor brought life to Cliveden. Her father-in-law had placed ancient Roman statues, busts and sarcophagi among Italian baroque tapestries and tooled and gilded leather walls. Declaring "the Astors have no taste," Nancy tossed out this "splendid gloom" and filled the house with chintzes and flowers. She also filled it with brilliant people, who were to become celebrated as "the Cliveden Set." Her equally spirited niece, Nancy Lancaster, recalled, "For evening amusements at Cliveden, there were charades and skits . . . Aunt Nannie did a very good hunting lady with the aid of false teeth, or a superb Charlie Chaplin."

In 1919 her husband inherited his father's peerage and gave up his seat in the House of Commons to join the House of Lords. Parliament had recently granted women the right to vote and sit in Parliament, so Lady Astor ran for her husband's seat. Noting that her Labour Party opponent was a conscientious objector, she opened her campaign with "If you want an MP who will be a repetition of the six hundred other MP's, don't elect me. If you want a lawyer, or if you want a pacifist, don't elect me. If you can't get a fighting man, take a fighting woman." Winning by a landslide, she became the first woman to sit in Parliament and an international symbol of feminism. She won six subsequent elections, serving for twenty-six years as a champion of women's rights, children's issues and temperance.

New Year's, New York

> *"Right after midnight it was everybody grabbing their coats, they couldn't wait to go on to the next party."*
>
> —ANDY WARHOL,
> *The Andy Warhol Diaries*,
> Friday, December 31, 1976

Andy Warhol, who designed a series of oh-so-stylishly whimsical Christmas and holiday greeting cards for Tiffany & Co. in the early 1960s, had a legendary love of New York parties of both the sumptuous and the fun-even-if-not-so-sumptuous varieties the city revels in.

This table set for a New Year's Eve supper, to be enjoyed by all before making the rounds of "after-midnight" happenings, is of the glitterati persuasion that Warhol embraced with "Oh gee! That's great!" enthusiasm.

Tiffany's vermeiled everything from "Chrysanthemum" flat silver to gadrooned service plates to set the luxuriant mood, while the black-and-gold porcelain dishes were designed by Tiffany's and handpainted in their Paris studios for the King of Saudi Arabia. To complete the table, an assortment of "Nuits de Chine" porcelain boxes is called into service to hold New Year's gifts at this quintessential "Nuit de New York."

The bright bouquet of anemones and the seriously night-blooming tablecloth are reminiscent of Andy Warhol's red rose, multicolor bird and star-spangled Tiffany greeting cards.

WHILE CHILDREN SLEEP

Hanging beside an elaborately detailed Regency rosewood chest, an embroidery of the regimental flags of the King's Own Borderers—with its assorted English lions joined by a white horse, an English rose and two Scotch thistle leaves doing their best for the season to look like holly, and all surrounded by a Scotch plaid check—would give this room an air of celebration appropriate to New Year's Eve even if there were no other ornaments.

With the cheerily and cavalierly masculine disregard for an orderly approach to interior furnishings, the room carries on in the spirit of the King's Own Borderers' curiously layered imagery.

Holly hangs from the robust William IV brass wall brackets, and the walls themselves maintain the Border feeling with their plaid covering. There is a paisley robe for the gentleman of the house and a silk patchwork lap rug for his lady.

Their gold-and-black papier-mâché supper table is set with Tiffany "Feathers" china, "Audubon"

flatware and "Honeycomb" English crystal. For additional merriment, there is champagne chilling in a gadroon-edged silver basin, while ornamental and Christmasy pink and green cabbages have taken up their position in a Tiffany Rouen-style faience wine cooler.

> " 'Mistletoe hung from the gas brackets in all the front parlours; there was sherry and walnuts and bottled beer and crackers by the dessert spoons . . .' "
>
> "I would sit among festoons and Chinese lanterns and nibble dates and try to make a model man-o'-war, following the Instructions for Little Engineers, and produce what might be mistaken for a sea-going tramcar."
>
> —DYLAN THOMAS,
> A Child's Christmas in Wales, 1950

A NEW ENGLAND HOLIDAY

*"But it's December the twenty-fourth,
and I am longing to be up north."*

—WHITE CHRISTMAS,
words and music by Irving Berlin, 1942

Santa Claus may be the only American whose tailoring has not been influenced by the knowing hand of "King of American Fashion" Bill Blass. His collections for both men and women have stayed at the forefront of American design for two generations, and no one is more familiar with the secrets of transforming the classic into the new with superbly tailored flair.

His genius for successfully mining America's rich affinity for English culture is here in all its quiet splendor in this setting for a New England holiday dinner. Every planned and polished detail of the late-eighteenth-century tavern building in northwestern Connecticut that Bill Blass has transformed into his country house speaks with Anglo-American authority.

The holiday meal to be served in the old tavern's half-paneled dining room reflects the restraint and classic simplicity of Colonial New England, where Christmas was never all tinsel and colored ornaments. The room's double-hung natural hard pine windows are surrounded with a handsome garland of pine boughs; and the typical Bill Blass country dinner prepared with traditional recipes carefully refined and perfected over the years will consist of meat loaf, baked russet potatoes and a colorfully layered vegetable terrine of carrots, mixed celery root and potatoes and finally broccoli, all seasoned with a bit of nutmeg and butter. This will be followed by a one-layer marmalade cake served with fresh whipped cream.

The bare polished wood dining table is set with Tiffany Italian country potteries from the town of

Este, south of Padua. There are green-and-white pierced-border service plates and trompe-l'oeil cabbage-leaf dinner plates. There is "King William" flat silver, first introduced by Tiffany & Co. in 1870, a restrained variation for the time on early-eighteenth-century English silver, from the William III period.

There are sparsely ornamented Tiffany "Classic" wineglasses and "Dionysus" Baccarat Bordeaux-bottle decanters, first designed for Tiffany & Co. by Bill Blass's late friend Van Day Truex, who was Design Director of Tiffany & Co. from 1955 until 1979, and a fellow champion of restraint.

Mr. Blass chooses not to use red or white flowers to decorate his holiday tables, but emulates a classic eighteenth-century New England country centerpiece with a silver Tiffany "Revere Bowl" filled with red apples and green pears.

The designer's fondness for meat loaf deserves special comment. Known in New York society as "designer meat loaf," the chili-sauce-, thyme-, marjoram- and celery-flavored mixture of beef, pork and veal makes much-applauded celebrity guest appearances on the menus of numerous fund-raising charity balls and is a staple on the menu of Glenn Bernbaum's Mortimer's, the favorite watering place of New York's elite. As Blass modestly says, "Everyone seems to like it."

The coffee and the marmalade cake, which waits on a footed crystal plate, will be served buffet-style from the room's side table, which in turn sits under a pair of monumental Tiffany silver five-armed candelabra placed in the windows for the occasion.

CHRISTMAS LUNCHEON AT STRATFIELD SAYE HOUSE

" 'There were the Useful Presents: engulfing mufflers of the old coach
days, and mittens made for giant sloths; zebra scarfs of a substance like
silky gum that could be tug-o'-warred down to the galoshes; blinding
tam-o'shanters like patchwork tea cozies and bunny-suited busbies and
balaclavas for victims of head-shrinking tribes . . . ' "

—DYLAN THOMAS,
A Child's Christmas in Wales, 1950

After Arthur Wellesley, 1st Duke of Wellington, defeated Napoleon at the Battle of Waterloo on the eighteenth of June, 1815, "the Iron Duke," as he was popularly known, was regarded as the savior of England. A grateful nation gave him £600,000 (a very large sum of money at the time) for the purchase of a house worthy of so great a military hero. In 1817, after considering architects' plans for various sprawling ducal affairs to be named Waterloo Palace, Wellington settled for the relatively modest Stratfield Saye House, which had been built around 1630 by Sir William Pitt, Comptroller of the Household of James I.

Wellington, being a practical man, was well satisfied with his convenient and comfortable house, to which he did add two comforts unheard of at the time, central heating and ample bathrooms. On a visit to Wellington in 1845, the twenty-six-year-old Queen Victoria noted that although she could not on the whole be enthusiastic about Wellington's lodging (she was used to the great ducal palaces of Marlborough's Blenheim and Devonshire's Chatsworth), she granted that it was "convenient, if rather hot."

Here at a Christmas lunch table set for the present and 8th Duke in the conservatory, the satinwood, mahogany and rosewood Regency table is furnished with Tiffany "Hampton" flat silver, "Napoleon Ivy" china, and goblets from Tiffany's Stately Homes Crystal Collection. A massive Tiffany cut-English-crystal footed bowl filled with pineapples and silvered Christmas tree ornaments centers the table.

The 8th Duke's menu includes asparagus mousse; roast turkey with chestnut stuffing; chipolata sausages and bacon rolls; brussels sprouts; roast potatoes; purée of carrots; bread sauce; Christmas pudding; mince pies; brandy butter; cream—all good traditional English dishes that both the 1st Duke and Queen Victoria would have recognized and approved.

The Duke's superb Regency upholstered tub chair in the Egyptian style, with its leopard mask arm supports and bronze-green-and-gilt finish, is reproduced in the Baker Furniture Stately Homes Collection from an original in Stratfield Saye's library, where the Iron Duke could often be found surrounded (in the room's showcases) by such eclectic mementos as two locks of hair, one from the head of George Washington (whose portrait by Gilbert Stuart also hangs in the library), the other from the mane of Copenhagen, Wellington's favorite chestnut stallion charger, which he rode throughout the Iberian Peninsular War against Napoleon's armies and at the Battle of Waterloo. Copenhagen later spent his last twenty-one years in retirement with Wellington and his family at Stratfield Saye.

The Wedgwood "Napoleon Ivy" dishes on the 8th Duke's table are a reflection of Wellington's lifelong fascination with his worthy adversary. This admiration is apparent again in the central hall and grand staircase of Apsley House, Wellington's palatial London residence, which is dominated by Antonio Canova's heroic white marble statue of Napoleon, as well as in Stratfield Saye's Print Room, which includes an engraving of the deposed Emperor of France gazing out to sea from his exile on St. Helena, which his admirer and adversary Wellington caused.

THE OLD YEAR PASSES

> *"In all the windows lights were shining and there was a glorious smell of roast goose, for it was New Year's Eve."*
>
> —HANS CHRISTIAN ANDERSEN,
> *The Little Match Girl*, 1848

The sideboard bouquets' branches of silvery money plant seedpods recall that to receive monies on the first, or "Hansel," Monday of January augurs well; but that to let money leave the house on New Year's Day suggests quite the opposite. Wise, if mercantile, thinking of this kind would already have noted that the lighting of fires (and wasting of resources) outdoors on December 31 was another ill-advised temptation of Fate.

Here, with the home fires blazing and with all the trappings and resources of great good fortune, Mrs. Frederic Bancroft's New Year's Eve table is set with Tiffany gold-and-white "Palmier d'Or" china; Tiffany "Hampton" vermeil flat silver; and "Newport" crystal. There is a footed Tiffany sterling silver goblet at each place to toast in the New Year.

The red-and-black-brocade-covered table is ornamented with simple but highly effective gilded pinecones and walnuts and a not-so-simple "Palmier d'Or" cachepot bursting with red berries mixed among white hothouse tulips, orchids, irises and roses. A "Nuit de Chine" patterned-porcelain Chinaman candlestick juggles red lacquer apples beneath the floral canopy of the centerpiece.

A "Palmier d'Or" coffee service, along with chilled champagne and a Tiffany regulator clock to strike midnight, waits on the eighteenth-century gilt marble-topped console sideboard; and the lady of the house has thrown her Christmas red Tiffany scarf printed with gold stars over the back of one of the room's gold-and-white Louis XVI armchairs.

For party favors, there is a Tiffany silver "shackle" keyring on each of the gentlemen's dinner napkins, and there is a Tiffany silver bow brooch on each of the ladies'.

The setting is grand enough for a dinner of three roast swans like those the Duke of Northumberland served at his New Year's dinner of 1512, as he noted in his *Household Book* of the same year. However, those days of profusion rather than refinement are long in the past, and today's New Year's dinners may center on a more classic roast goose, as in Scandinavia or Central Europe; or grilled white sausage, or *boudin blanc*, with grilled pineapple slices, as in France; or *cotechino* and *zampone* sausages with beans or lentils, as in Italy. Or perhaps it will recall New Orleans with a gumbo made with shrimp and crabmeat or chicken, along with a *daube glacée*, that simple and excellent boiled beef larded with cayenne-seasoned salt pork and flavored with thyme, bay, parsley, onion, carrots, garlic and sherry and simmered for four hours with calfs' and pigs' feet and then chilled and jellied before serving.

As this is a most citified dinner, the old country custom of opening all the doors a few minutes before midnight—for "letting the old year out and the new year in"—may not be observed. The men may, however, think of a variant of the old Italian custom of selling the first drink of the New Year for a kiss. Or, as New Year's is the favored season for divinations, there may be all manner of fortune-telling and "other Gaelic customs, relative to the eve of the New Year," as noted by T. G. Crippen in his 1923 compilation *Christmas and Christmas Lore*, that are "survivals of heathenism" and "need not be further enlarged on."

NEW YEAR'S AT NEWPORT

No American houses were ever so gilded, so shamelessly extravagant, so theatrical in the near madness of their architectural fancies and in their borrowings from the grandeurs of European palaces as the "cottages" of Newport; and no parties were ever so intricate and ornate in their concept and in their décor, or so blatantly ostentatious, as the fêtes held in these glittering cottages' great halls and ballrooms.

Since the first of these legendary celebrations, a fête champêtre hosted in 1857 by China Trade king William Shepard Wetmore at his new Italianate villa, Château-sur-Mer, where he received three thousand guests, the pace of festivities has seldom slowed in this privileged summer colony so "magnificently unconcerned with reality"–to borrow a phrase from Vincent Scully.

In the latter part of the nineteenth century and at the beginning of the twentieth, the Wetmores' Château-sur-Mer was to be eclipsed on Bellevue Avenue and Ocean Drive by vast neo-Gothic, neobaroque, neoclassic, neorococo and neo-mixture-of-everything cottages of a pomp and luxury never again equaled in America, or elsewhere for that matter.

One after another the cottage palaces went up for the incalculably rich: the William K. Vanderbilts' glistening and generously gilded Marble House, designed by Richard Morris Hunt; New York real estate tycoon Ogden Goelet's neo–French Renaissance Ochre Court and Cornelius Vanderbilt II's dauntingly and unabashedly splendid seventy-room neo–Italian Renaissance palazzo, The Breakers (both also by Hunt); coal king Edward Julius Berwind's rococo and grandiose château, The Elms; and McKim, Mead & White's masterpiece, the Hermann Oelrichs's Rosecliff, modeled on Louis XIV's Grand Trianon at Versailles.

The parties were no more modest than the cottages. There was the Bal Blanc of Mrs. Oelrichs, the Comstock Lode silver heiress, on August 19, 1904, when the vestibule and ballroom of Rosecliff were turned into a garden of massed white hollyhocks, hydrangeas, roses, orchids and lilies of the valley, and when the women wore only white and powdered their hair. There was the combined coming-out party for Gertrude Vanderbilt and housewarming of The Breakers for six hundred guests in August 1895, an event whose centenary was commemorated by her family with a dinner dance on July 22, 1995, for the same number, which still included several dozen Vanderbilts.

There was Gertrude Vanderbilt's cousin Consuelo Vanderbilt's coming-out party, also in August of 1895, attended this time by only five hundred guests, among them the 9th Duke of Marlborough, who was so impressed by the carryings-on that he proposed to the eighteen-year-old debutante that evening in Marble House's Gothic Room.

Here, for a New Year's Eve dinner dance in the grand Newport style, the table is ornamented with a pair of heroically proportioned Tiffany Venetian glass candlesticks recalling the balusters of Venetian rococo palaces. There are oversized crystal beakers to hold individual carafes of iced vodka, Tiffany "Palmette" flat silver and "Provence" stemware.

The mixed gold-toned architectural details and redolent cabbage roses of the room's curtains and table cover recall the high neobaroque style of turn-of-the-century Newport.

> "... snow grew overnight on the roofs of the houses like a pure and grandfather moss, minutely white-ivied the walls and settled on the postman, opening the gate, like a dumb, numb thunderstorm of white, torn Christmas cards."
>
> —DYLAN THOMAS,
> *A Child's Christmas in Wales*, 1950

DECEMBER 31

The fashion for Louis XVI furniture was introduced to the United States by Mrs. William K. Vanderbilt, who in 1877 commissioned famed architect Richard Morris Hunt to design her and her husband's French Renaissance–style mansion at the northwest corner of Fifth Avenue and Fifty-second Street in New York. When it was completed in 1881, the pale, delicately carved limestone exterior made the heavy brownstone exteriors of other New York houses seem quite dull by comparison. The Régence–Louis XV–style salon, designed and executed by the decorating firm of Allard & Fils of Paris, had cream-painted boiseries with gilt moldings, tapestries after cartoons by Francois Boucher, a *parquet de Versailles* floor and a circular ceiling painting in the style of the eighteenth-century Venetian painter Giovanni Battista Tiepolo by Paris society muralist of talent Paul Baudry. This spacious, airy room sparkling with gilt made other "artistic" New York interiors of the 1880s seem stiff and rather poor.

In the fall of 1882, Mrs. Vanderbilt's footmen cautiously placed two of the world's most valuable and extraordinary pieces of furniture beneath the salon's Boucher tapestries. Jean Henri Riesener, the great French *ébéniste*, had made both a massive ormolu-mounted and marble-topped ebony commode and a matching *secrétaire à abattant* for Marie Antoinette in 1785. They incorporated exquisite black-and-gold Japanese lacquer panels of birds, plants and landscapes, which Riesener mounted with sumptuous, exquisitely finished gilt-bronze garlands and friezes bearing the cipher "MA." Mrs. Vanderbilt's agents in London had purchased these marvels, which are now in the collections of the Metropolitan Museum of Art, at Christie's auction of the Duke of Hamilton's collection, on July 10, 1882, for £19,900, then equivalent to $94,500.

No one else in America had furniture remotely equaling the Vanderbilts' Riesener commode and *secrétaire*, and "Louis XVI envy" incited America's most social and powerful capitalists to collect this last grand style of France's ancien régime. The leader of the craze was no less than J. Pierpont Morgan.

Up-to-date Americans who were less prodigiously rich filled their cream-and-gilt salons with lesser Louis XVI furniture, or with furniture purported to be of the Louis XVI period. By the 1910s, suites of matching settees, bergères and fauteuils had proliferated in antique dealers' showrooms as if by magic, and the most highly prized were upholstered in Vanderbilt style with Boucher-type tapestries.

Here, demonstrating that the New York taste for Louis XVI furniture has never gone out of fashion, two fine and authentic, if unmatched, Louis XVI tapestry-covered *fauteuils à la reine* are drawn up to this New Year's Eve supper table, covered with a boldly patterned and colored floral chintz tablecloth and set with equally bold Tiffany "Flames" Italian ceramic service plates.

There is Tiffany "Chrysanthemum" flat silver designed in 1880 and in use by the time of the opening of the W. K. Vanderbilt house in 1881; and there are Tiffany "Luciano" water goblets, champagne flutes and claret glasses; apple-shaped silver boxes; a Tiffany Louis XIV–style vermeil four-branched candelabrum; and a pair of Tiffany English Regency–style "Palm Tree" vermeil candlesticks to add to the air of lavish eclectic elegance. To the side, an eighteenth-century Italian gilt-and-lacquered credenza holds a silver tray set with Tiffany "Yellow Strip" ceramic coffee cups and a Tiffany Georgian–style sterling silver coffee pot.

> *"Yes, those were really quite happy times!*
> *. . . he told of the Christmas Eve, when*
> *he had been hung with sweetmeats*
> *and candles."*
>
> —HANS CHRISTIAN ANDERSEN,
> *The Fir Tree,* 1846

GOLD-AND-WHITE DINNER

At Tiffany & Co., all that glitters is gold, unless of course it turns out to be a diamond or maybe a ruby, emerald or sapphire. This dependable rule of thumb has already drawn eight generations of shoppers during the holiday seasons, which unfailingly reanimate faith in the pleasant art of giving.

As early as 1869, the *New York Dispatch* noted in its December 12 issue:

The approach of Christmas and New Year season is welcomed by young and old as a time for interchanging those tokens of kindness which, whatever be their intrinsic value, are inestimable as gauges of family union and tributes of friendly esteem.

Our great bazaar of Broadway is becoming more animated daily with the concourse of gift-buyers, providing themselves with charming little *"surprises"*; and whether we survey some group of enthusiastic ladies exploring Tiffany's varied collection of all that can gratify refined taste, while a virtuoso near by pauses in his inspection of some rare bronzes or exquisite cameos, to catch their piquant exclamations of delight; or whether we mark some face peeping into the window, with eager wishfulness in its admiring expression—we may be sure that the sweet holiday desire to buy something for somebody, is nestling in the hearts of all of them. We never glance into Tiffany's ourselves without wishing to possess a Fortunatus purse of gold, and straightway buy a thousand beautiful things, wherewith to gladden a thousand households . . .

The Diamond kings, Messrs. Tiffany & Co. [the *Dispatch* went on to note some days later], are among the wonders of New York, and whose superb specimens of American workmanship do so much credit to the skill and taste of our national designers and artisans, excel themselves in their array of rich and costly articles for the present year.

Their magnificent stock embracing values of $1,500,000, is displayed in combinations of splendor in the pieces themselves without the aid of meretricious outside adornments, that would awaken the envy of the old time Caliphs of Bagdad.

During all the fair weather of the past week, the beautiful Broadway front of their *magasin* has witnessed throngs of waiting carriages and hurrying customers, from 9 a.m. until after sundown, while inside the spaces between the show cases were almost impassable for the eager multitude of retail purchasers. There the spectacle is one that could not be accurately described without the appearance of exaggeration.

In this unrivaled assortment, variety vies with beauty, utility, and costliness.

Every region of the earth, every realm of nature, and every turn of thought has, in a word, contributed to this magical display, and the stranger can find no fairer starting point for a correct estimate of the wealth and taste that preside over trade in the Great Metropolis, than at No. 550 and 552 Broadway, where the Genii of Oriental romance seem to have appointed their rendezvous for the Holidays of 1869–70.

Here at a setting for the holidays of over one hundred years later, a Tiffany table is still prepared to awaken the appetite and perhaps "the envy of the old time Caliphs of Bagdad" with its "English King" vermeil silverware, its "Feathers" china, its "Tiffany Swag" crystal stemware and its centerpiece of mirrored Christmas tree balls that glitter but—alas!—are not gold.

"The pies were great—apple, mince and plum. The turkey had already been cut up like a magazine would tell you to before it got to the table, so it was like a Turkey Puzzle."

—ANDY WARHOL,
The Andy Warhol Diaries,
Saturday, December 25, 1976

A VENETIAN BALL

The decorative arts of Venice, the glorious glasswares of the Venetian island of Murano and the so sophisticated ceramics of the Veneto, of Este and of Nove, have long been the jewels of Tiffany table furnishings.

Murano glass was originally introduced to the United States by Tiffany & Co. Their *New York Times* advertisement of November 16, 1869, read, "Tiffany & Co. are opening daily their Importations for the Holidays—Venetian Glass. A small collection of this rare and beautiful glass of the style of the XVI century. Enamelled, filigree and colored thread. Vases, Coups, Ewers, Bottles, Boudoir Mirrors, the first offered for sale in this country, just received."

Shortly after, in their issue of December 18, 1869, the *Times* commented on these marvels new to America:

> Tiffany & Co. . . . have also a supply monopoly, the only one in this country, being the only importer here of the peculiar Venetian glass, the artistic making and tinting which, once lost, has lately been restored by Salviati of Venice.
>
> They have a very superior stock of vases in the Byzantine and other styles which are gotten up in the highest style of art.
>
> Near everything, in fact, suitable for holiday presents may be found in this establishment, the interior of which, in the way of costly adornments, reminds one of some fabled grotto of the Orient rather than of a store on Broadway.

Tiffany's settings of Venetian glass may still "remind one of some fabled grotto of the Orient," but it is now the Murano glasshouse of Archimede Seguso, the world-renowned master of his craft, that has supplied Tiffany's for over forty years.

The "artistic making and tinting" was never "once lost," not for an instant. Glass of consummate craftsmanship has been produced without interruption on the island of Murano by the Seguso family and others for almost seven centuries, and Tiffany's has been presenting it to the American public for almost one hundred thirty years.

Just as Venetian glass plays no small part in the fabled balls that are still given in the flamboyantly extravagant interiors of Venice's Gothic, baroque and rococo palaces, it plays no small part in Tiffany table settings.

The Venetians have no special fondness for massings of flowers on their dinner tables; rather, they prefer what they refer to as *giardini*, gardens made of miniature ceramic or crystal ornaments, columns, statues, and topiary shapes. Some may hold candles, some not. The *giardini* may then be accented with tiny bouquets of flowers or of boxwood or ivy, but flowers' or greenery's role is usually small.

Here in a Venetian ballroom Christmastime table setting worthy of the legendary parties of the Palazzo Labia, or of the Ca' Rezzonico, or of the Albrizzi, Pisani-Moretti and Zenobio palazzi, the table, set with Tiffany "American Garden" flat silver, "Nemours" stemware, and Sybil Connolly–designed "Merrion Square" china, is furnished with a *giardino* of Archimede Seguso's glass ornaments, which include three festive and spiraling red, clear and blue "Carnival" flame candleholders, along with a clear-glass dolphin that is also very much in a festive carnival mood. These are anchored by a towering two-foot-tall baluster column candlestick, which, like all the table's small miracles of Venice, is "rare and beautiful" and "gotten up in the highest style of art."

> "... *every net was filled with sweetmeats; golden apples and walnuts hung down as if they grew there, and more than a hundred little candles, red, white and blue, were fastened to the different boughs.*"
>
> —HANS CHRISTIAN ANDERSEN,
> *The Fir Tree*, 1846

FÊTE ORIENTALE

Throughout the middle of the nineteenth century, much of Tiffany design conformed to the Victorian spirit of realism and its Romantic vision of nature; however, with the opening of trade with Japan by Commodore Perry on March 31, 1854, Tiffany design looked to the Pacific Basin and discovered Japanese art, and especially Japanese woodcuts, scroll paintings and figured textiles, with their free and open naturalism and more abstract and highly manipulated concept of nature, quite in keeping with Tiffany and American designs' quest for clarity.

Under the leadership of head designer Edward C. Moore, Tiffany's made Japonism its own with its great body of "Japanesque" silverware design, which remains one of Tiffany and American designs' better achievements. Tiffany's 1871 "Audubon" flat silver is a best-seller to this day, and Japonism's influence on Tiffany's contemporary design, such as its recent flat silver pattern "American Garden," is marked.

Here at a holiday dinner for two given by the ever stylish Mrs. John W. Anderson II of Bermuda and Palm Beach, bright-red-and-gold Japanese furnishings set the Christmas season mood. The table is covered with an antique-gold-and-blue-brocade obi and set with Tiffany black-and-gold "Nuit de Chine" Paris porcelain, which, despite its name and like so much French chinoiserie, is inspired by the black-and-gold lacquers of Japan.

The red-and-white oriental pheasant is pleased to know that turkey is on the Christmas menu.

> *"Everything was great, though, it was the best turkey and everything was fresh, the peas and everything, so I porked it up."*
>
> —ANDY WARHOL,
> *The Andy Warhol Diaries,*
> Wednesday, December 24, 1980

THE NEW YEAR ENTERS

> *"Bring her the loveliest rose in the world,*
> *the one which is the expression of the*
> *brightest and purest love . . ."*
>
> —HANS CHRISTIAN ANDERSEN,
> *The Loveliest Rose in the World*, 1852

Throughout her career as food critic of the *New York Times* and *Time* magazine, columnist at *Condé Nast Traveler* and author of *Visions of Sugarplums*, *From My Mother's Kitchen* and *New York's Best Restaurants*, Mimi Sheraton—with her outspokenness, her trenchant honesty and her infectious, joyful enthusiasm—has remained America's both best-loved and most controversial restaurant critic.

Every New Year's Day, she and husband Richard Falcone receive friends—all "Green Berets among eaters," she might say—at a holiday smorgasbord in their charm-filled 1852 Manhattan townhouse.

The table is always decked with a long red damask cloth and a huge bowl of holly and red red roses, whose colors are echoed by the leaves and red ribbons of "Tiffany Garland" holiday china.

There is always bright orange gravlax with mustard sauce, many and varied fish salads, Swedish meatballs and a baked Polish ham. The architectural Danish holiday cake will sport little paper Danish and American flags to wish everyone a Happy New Year and "a never-ending bon appétit."

TWELFTH NIGHT

"May each Christmas, as it comes, find us . . . more simple-minded, more humble, more affectionate . . . more happy."

—JOHN HENRY CARDINAL NEWMAN, *A Christmas Prayer,* c. 1850

The Twelfth Day of Christmas brings the conclusion of the holiday season on January 6. This is "Old Christmas," the evening of the arrival of the Three Kings and the gifts of gold, frankincense and myrrh.

The Christmas tree, with all its glittering tinsel, its blizzard of colored ornaments of every possible and impossible description and its twinkle of lights, comes down, but the natural sense of wonder and goodwill that the holidays inspire reigns for a final evening of celebration, and often of more gifts.

Green is now the color of the feast, and the table is set with golden Tiffany "Bamboo" vermeil and with silver and vermeil-covered apple bowls. Dinner will end with a ground-almond-cream-filled *galette des Rois* to honor the Three Kings, and whoever finds the dried bean hidden inside will wear a gilt paper crown and be king or queen for the day.

Here a majestic white hart already reigns over the evening wearing a royal crown of his own; and if this is a traditional French Twelfth Night, or *fête des Rois,* there are thirteen desserts—the *galette* plus twelve more—to mark the Three Kings' twelve-day journey to Bethlehem and the grand finale of Christmas.

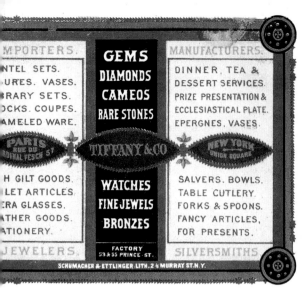

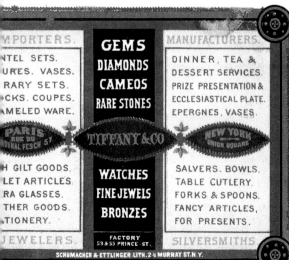
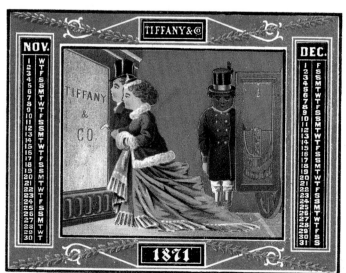